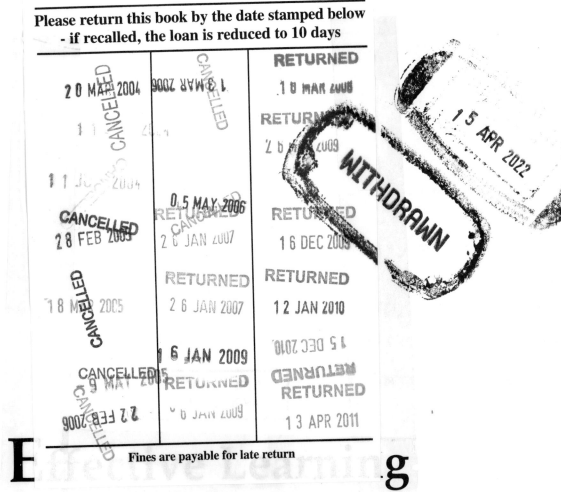
Effective Learning

in
Science

Keith Bishop
&
Paul Denley

D0241537

Published by Network Educational Press Ltd.
PO Box 635
Stafford
ST16 1BF

First Published 1997
© Keith Bishop & Paul Denley 1997

ISBN 1 85539 039 6

Series Editor - Professor Tim Brighouse
Edited by Sara Peach & Carol Thompson
Design & layout by
Neil Hawkins of Devine Design
Illustrations by Joe Rice

Printed in Great Britain by
Redwood Books, Trowbridge, Wilts.

Foreword

A teacher's task is much more ambitious than it used to be and demands a focus on the subtleties of teaching and learning and on the emerging knowledge of school improvement.

This is what this series is about.

Teaching can be a very lonely activity. The time honoured practice of a single teacher working alone in the classroom is still the norm; yet to operate alone is, in the end to become isolated and impoverished. This series addresses two issues – the need to focus on practical and useful ideas connected with teaching and learning and the wish thereby to provide some sort of an antidote to the loneliness of the long distance teacher who is daily berated by an anxious society.

Teachers flourish best when, in key stage teams or departments (or more rarely whole schools), their talk is predominantly about teaching and learning and where, unconnected with appraisal, they are privileged to observe each other teach; to plan and review their work together; and to practise the habit of learning from each other new teaching techniques. But how does this state of affairs arise? Is it to do with the way staffrooms are physically organised so that the walls bear testimony to interesting articles and in the corner there is a dedicated computer tuned to 'conferences' about SEN, school improvement, the teaching of English etc., and whether, in consequence, the teacher leaning over the shoulder of the enthusiastic IT colleagues sees the promise of interesting practice elsewhere? Has the primary school cracked it when it organises successive staff meetings in different classrooms and invites the 'host' teacher to start the meeting with a 15 minute exposition of their classroom organisation and management? Or is it the same staff sharing, on a rota basis, a slot on successive staff meeting agenda when each in turn reviews a new book they have used with their class? And what of the whole school which now uses 'active' and 'passive' concerts of carefully chosen music as part of their accelerated learning techniques?

It is of course well understood that excellent teachers feel threatened when first they are observed. Hence the epidemic of trauma associated with OFSTED. The constant observation of the teacher in training seems like that of the learner driver. Once you have passed your test and can drive unaccompanied, you do. You often make lots of mistakes and sometimes get into bad habits. Woe betide, however, the back seat driver who tells you so. In the same way the new teacher quickly loses the habit of observing others and being observed. So how do we get a confident, mutual observation debate going? One school I know found a simple and therefore brilliant solution. The Head of the History Department asked that a young colleague plan lessons for her – the Head of Department – to teach. This lesson she then taught, and was observed by the young colleague. There was subsequent discussion, in which the young teacher asked,

> *"Why did you divert the question and answer session I had planned?"*
> and was answered by,
> *"Because I could see that I needed to arrest the attention of the group by the window with some "hands-on" role play, etc."*

This lasted an hour and led to a once-a-term repeat discussion which, in the end, was adopted by the whole school. The whole school subsequently changed the pattern of its meetings to consolidate extended debate about teaching and learning. The two teachers claimed that because one planned and the other taught both were implicated but neither alone was responsible or felt 'got at'.

So there are practices which are both practical and more likely to make teaching a rewarding and successful activity. They can, as it were, increase the likelihood of a teacher surprising the pupils into understanding or doing something they did not think they could do rather than simply entertaining them or worse still occupying them. There are ways of helping teachers judge the best method of getting pupil expectation just ahead of self-esteem.

This series focuses on straightforward interventions which individual schools and teachers use to make life more rewarding for themselves and those they teach. Teachers deserve nothing less, for they are the architects of tomorrow's society, and society's ambition for what they achieve increases as each year passes.

Professor Tim Brighouse.

Contents

What this book is about

There has been growing interest over the last few years in the general concept of educational effectiveness. Initially the term was applied to schools themselves and a 'school effectiveness movement' has grown up, concerned principally with improving the performance of schools, as measured by externally recognised performance indicators such as national test or examination results.

As the movement developed, the term 'school improvement' has also come into common usage, suggesting that the issue is not just about measuring the effectiveness of schools, but more importantly attempting to make them more effective. The initial focus on whole schools has since moved to considering in more detail different levels within the school. So attempts have been made to characterise the 'effective department' and the 'effective teacher'. This brings us closer to the classroom and to what we mean by 'effective teaching' and 'effective learning' and the relationship between the two.

So what is the relationship between effective teaching and effective learning? Are they two sides of the same coin? Teaching could be judged to be effective if it results in effective learning but it is not that simple! It is very difficult (if not impossible) to guarantee learning will follow – no matter how good our teaching. Learning is an active process involving at least one human being – and human beings, particularly young ones, are at times unpredictable, influenced by feelings and above all, different from one another. The best we can hope to do is to increase the probability that learning will take place, by creating the right conditions and by supporting the process as best we can. These elements of effectiveness are the subject of this book.

We are concerned principally with these three questions:

- **What is effective learning in the context of science?**
- **How can you plan to encourage it?**
- **How can you support it in the classroom?**

The first two sections of this book address the first of these questions. Section One will look at it from the pupils' point of view by considering several perspectives on what is likely to make them effective learners. Then, in Section Two we will consider some of the aims and purposes of teaching science. It is important to start with a clear view about this if we are to make judgements about what 'effective' means. We will also think about the role of subject knowledge in effective teaching.

Section Three encourages you to review what is going on at the moment through a 'departmental audit', focusing on three areas – views you hold about teaching science, an evaluation of your current schemes of work, and pupils' perspectives.

Section Four tackles a number of issues concerning planning for effective learning, particularly the development of schemes of work built around the principles outlined in Sections One and Two.

The third of the above questions is addressed by Section Five which looks at the use of resources to support effective learning, and Section Six which mainly considers management issues.

At the end of Sections Two, Four, Five and Six there are a number of Professional Development Activities to aid the process of evaluating current practice and planning developments for the future.

There is a short Afterword which is concerned with the development of a departmental plan to revise schemes of work, resources or classroom strategies in order to make learning and teaching more effective. This is followed by a selective Bibliography.

In the Appendix, at the end of the book, there is a selection of material which can be photoreproduced for use in development activities or as overhead transparencies.

Anglocentrism warning!
The context with which we are most familiar is the educational system in England with its National Curriculum, OFSTED and the DfEE. However, we hope that readers in other parts of the UK or further afield will see that the basic messages in this book about effective learning in science apply fairly widely to schools and educational systems in many areas, and will forgive any unintentional impression of Anglocentrism. We do understand that the National Curriculum only applies to maintained schools in England and Wales; the situation in Northern Ireland is slightly different and we recognise the very different set-up in Scotland. We try, where possible, to acknowledge the differences and indeed with reference to Scotland are considerably encouraged by the approach to future development of the science curriculum.

We have four personal aims for this book which we hope will distinguish it from related publications. These are:

- **to help departments integrate a number of different influences in picturing what effective learning means for them;**

- **to argue for a more sophisticated approach to developing schemes of work that have greater potential to match learners' needs;**

- **to show that ideas about effective learning are easier to address if we move away from dividing our teaching up into short 'lessons' and towards thinking about 'learning cycles' within a longer timescale;**

- **to encourage science departments to exploit the professional development opportunities in a collaborative approach to curriculum planning.**

OHT1

Effective learning is a multivariate problem – tackling it is rather like eating an elephant! "How do you that?" The answer is … "In small bites!"

This book should help you identify which bit of the elephant you are going to attack first and what cutlery to use!!

How to use this book

The book has been written for the Head of Science or the second in department who is interested in taking a look at the effectiveness of teaching and learning.

The emphasis is on a departmental approach to these issues and working collaboratively towards shared goals.

The book is intended to support this aim by providing practical ideas for development based on good practice or research perspectives, complemented by activities which could take place through in-service days or departmental meetings.

Many of the illustrations and summaries could easily be turned into overhead projector transparencies for use on such occasions using an enlarging photocopier. These have been indicated by the symbol shown on the right, and can also be found in the appendix at the back of the book.

OHT

In a book of this length, we cannot explore all the issues fully so we have included a bibliography to suggest sources of further reading. We have referred to sources which we feel science departments will find useful in following up ideas. It is a sad sign of the (financial) times that many science departments do not have their own libraries of books about teaching science or they contain very dated collections of books. Heads of Science might think creatively about trying to use INSET funding to build up such collections for the further professional development of staff. There will be a stronger case if this is linked to school or departmental development planning or to an action plan following a school inspection. We have resisted referring to journals on the grounds that they may not be easy to access, although many of the books in the bibliography provide further references of this sort.

It is not necessary to read the book from beginning to end.

The 'audit' activities in Section Three are designed to provide an indication of potential areas for further development. If you are interested in schemes of work then you will go to Section Four but you could be more interested in classroom approaches in Section Six or resource issues in Section Five. Whatever you focus on, the final section will be useful in producing a realistic development plan for the areas you decide to concentrate on first.

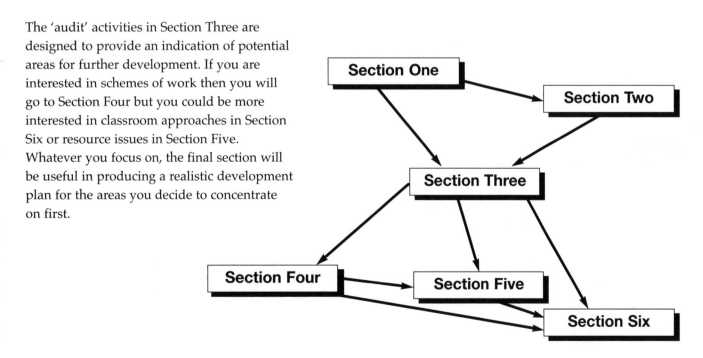

What is 'effective learning' in science?

The purposes of this section are all related to our understanding of what constitutes effective learning from the viewpoint of the learner. There is not necessarily only one way of looking at this and it will be important to establish a shared vision. To achieve this, this section will ...

● **consider ways in which children's learning can be maximised**
● **introduce a number of influences which may be significant in effective learning**
● **develop a set of principles which might reflect good practice**

These quotes give a starting point:

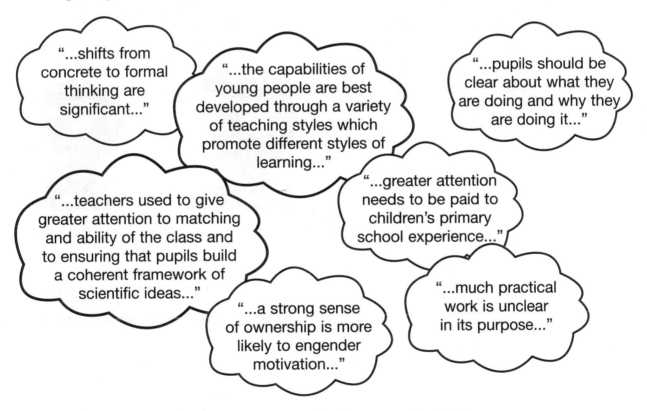

The title of this book begs the obvious question – what do we mean by effective learning? We can think about this question from at least two points of view:

● Learning is effective if children are learning to their maximum potential.

   or

● Learning is effective if children are learning what we want them to learn.

The first of these responses considers learning from the learner's viewpoint and may be more interested in the *process* of learning than its content. The second looks at things more from our viewpoint as teachers of science and where concerns might be more with the content.

Clearly these two viewpoints are closely interrelated. It would be hard to consider the question of effective learning without some reference to both the learner and the subject being studied. Learning is unlikely to be effective if the content is not matched to the learner's needs. (We will consider the question of what we might want children to learn in Section Two).

The purpose of this section is to consider the first perspective – what should we be doing to *maximise the learner's potential for learning?* We will explore recent research and practice to identify ideas which help to achieve this. Considering these ideas can increase the probability of effective learning taking place; several are related to teaching approaches. At the end of the section we will draw from them some of the characteristics of effective learning.

1 Recognising children's ideas in science

The Children's Learning in Science project (CLIS) in this country and hundreds of other studies worldwide show that children do not come to science lessons with empty heads. Instead, they arrive with ideas about science, many of them misconceived, which they have gathered from parents, friends, television, magazines and so on. On entering their science lessons it cannot be assumed they will put those alternative ideas to one side and gratefully assimilate the accepted scientific explanations.

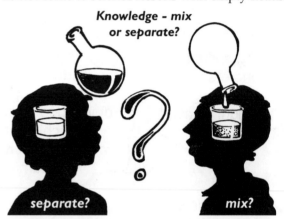

Knowledge - mix or separate?

separate? *mix?*

Misconceptions

The research shows that a number of things can happen. Some children simply mix the school science with what's already in their heads, resulting in a concoction of intended and unintended meanings. Others do not build in the accepted scientific ideas at all. Others hold both sets of ideas quite happily even when they contradict one another.

A recent discussion paper from the Scottish Consultative Council for the Curriculum puts this quite clearly:

> *Effective teaching of science depends to a considerable extent on the adoption of views of learning which recognise and value each person's existing ideas and beliefs and the active role played by learners when they are developing their understanding of scientific ideas and explanations. ... Clearly, this has implications for the teaching of science ... and the roles teachers play in this process.*

Science Education in Scottish Schools *(SCCC, 1996)*

This statement echoes what was contained in guidance from both the National Curriculum Council in England and the Curriculum Council for Wales when the National Curriculum was introduced. Research shows that understanding in science is more likely to occur when pupils are helped to recognise their alternative ideas. The teaching should then provide them with active opportunities to reconstruct new meanings by modifying or abandoning existing ideas. The starting point for teaching is therefore taking into account any prior learning and eliciting pupils' ideas –

i.e. 'beginning where the children are'. This approach might worry some teachers as they argue that the exposure of pupils to a range of conflicting ideas will compound the confusion. However the research is clear. Firstly, children when given the opportunity, are prepared to compare their scientific ideas with those of other children. Secondly, they are willing to modify those ideas as a result of the teaching they receive, when their alternative frameworks (as they are sometimes called) fail to explain satisfactorily what they see. In the words of the American psychologist, David Ausubel:

> *The most important single factor influencing learning is what the learner already knows. Ascertain this and teach him (sic) accordingly.*

The notion that learners construct and restructure their ideas leads this approach to learning to be called the 'constructivist' view of learning. The summary below characterises this view:

- **Learning outcomes depend not only on the learning environment but also the knowledge of the learner.**
- **Learning involves the construction of meanings. Meanings constructed by pupils from what they see or hear may not be those intended. Construction of a meaning is influenced to a large extent by their existing knowledge.**
- **The construction of meaning is a continuous and active process.**
- **Meanings, once constructed, are evaluated and can be accepted or rejected.**
- **Learners have the final responsibility for their learning.**

OHT2

Interactive Teaching in Science (*Children's Learning in Science project, University of Leeds, 1990*)

During the 1980s, practising science teachers worked with the CLIS team at the University of Leeds to develop teaching schemes in the areas of energy, particle theory and plant nutrition. The team developed a generalised model for teaching, shown over the page.

We will return to this model in Section Six. The message from the research is clear. Effective science teaching must recognise and elicit pupils' 'alternative frameworks' through a wide range of activities which pick up on their common misconceptions. These establish pupils' starting points and give them the opportunity to bring into conscious thought ideas which they have never had to articulate clearly before. Brief question and answer sessions will not necessarily do this. The teacher requires a more elaborate range of methods involving pupils in activities such as:

- Producing posters to answer questions such as "How does electricity flow round a circuit?"
- Making concept maps to show relationships between ideas about how plants feed
- Sorting cards with names of common substances into piles of solids, liquids and gases
- Completing questionnaires about which human characteristics can be inherited
- A circus of simple practical experiments to investigate floating and sinking

OHT3

A model for teaching

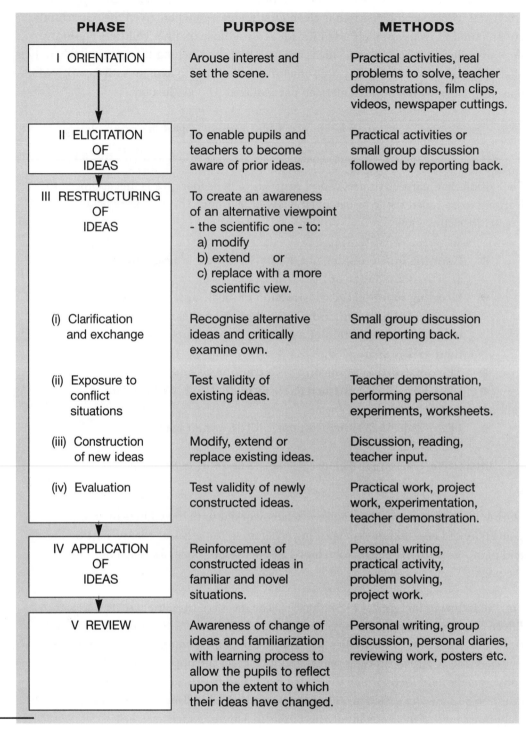

PHASE	PURPOSE	METHODS
I ORIENTATION	Arouse interest and set the scene.	Practical activities, real problems to solve, teacher demonstrations, film clips, videos, newspaper cuttings.
II ELICITATION OF IDEAS	To enable pupils and teachers to become aware of prior ideas.	Practical activities or small group discussion followed by reporting back.
III RESTRUCTURING OF IDEAS	To create an awareness of an alternative viewpoint - the scientific one - to: a) modify b) extend or c) replace with a more scientific view.	
(i) Clarification and exchange	Recognise alternative ideas and critically examine own.	Small group discussion and reporting back.
(ii) Exposure to conflict situations	Test validity of existing ideas.	Teacher demonstration, performing personal experiments, worksheets.
(iii) Construction of new ideas	Modify, extend or replace existing ideas.	Discussion, reading, teacher input.
(iv) Evaluation	Test validity of newly constructed ideas.	Practical work, project work, experimentation, teacher demonstration.
IV APPLICATION OF IDEAS	Reinforcement of constructed ideas in familiar and novel situations.	Personal writing, practical activity, problem solving, project work.
V REVIEW	Awareness of change of ideas and familiarization with learning process to allow the pupils to reflect upon the extent to which their ideas have changed.	Personal writing, group discussion, personal diaries, reviewing work, posters etc.

OHT4

CLIS, University of Leeds

Of course, identification of the misconceptions is only the beginning. The teacher needs to devise activities to challenge pupils' alternative frameworks and help them actively construct new meanings which incorporate the accepted scientific view. Sometimes children's ideas are deeply held and hard to shift; on other occasions an appropriate question can cause the children themselves to change their ideas.

This process involves 'cognitive conflict' – placing pupils in situations where an idea is challenged in a way which makes them think about its adequacy and encourages them

Effective Learning in Science

to think about changing it. Learning depends on the pupil actively reconstructing meaning because the 'alternative framework' cannot answer the question.

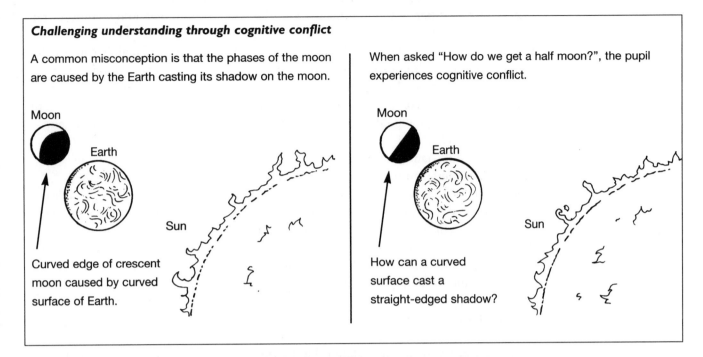

Challenging understanding through cognitive conflict

A common misconception is that the phases of the moon are caused by the Earth casting its shadow on the moon.

Moon

Earth

Sun

Curved edge of crescent moon caused by curved surface of Earth.

When asked "How do we get a half moon?", the pupil experiences cognitive conflict.

Moon

Earth

Sun

How can a curved surface cast a straight-edged shadow?

There are many books in this area of research but **'Making Sense of Secondary Science'**, *R Driver et al. (Routledge, 1994)* (see Bibliography p.97), is a good starting point for further references to a whole variety of misconceptions in every area of the curriculum.

There are wide-ranging implications from this research. It suggests that we are trying to teach too many high-level concepts without giving pupils the opportunity to develop ideas for themselves. The curriculum is overloaded so we may feel we do not have the time to do this, but without giving them these opportunities the evidence is that pupils may return to their 'wrong' ideas. In other words, they do not learn the accepted scientific ideas that we want them to learn. The pupils have not integrated these ideas and their understanding remains unreconstructed. This is highlighted in a recent report from OFSTED:

> *Most pupils acquire a sound factual knowledge of the material in the Programme of Study but their understanding of the underlying scientific concepts often remains fragmentary. ... as the content of science becomes conceptually more demanding, there is a progressive polarisation of pupils' achievement, with the least able often becoming confused and holding incorrect ideas.*

Subjects and Standards *(HMSO, 1996)*

This judgement is a cause for concern and reinforces what the examined research tells us: we must look carefully at both curriculum content and the way we teach if the learning of science is to be effective.

2 **Reinforcing the inter-relationship between procedural and conceptual understanding**

The National Curriculum for Science in England and Wales is intended to enable pupils to develop two different but interrelated forms of scientific understanding – **procedural** and **conceptual**. The Programmes of Study for the first attainment target – often referred to as Sc1 – relate to 'Experimental and Investigative Science' and are mainly concerned with developing an understanding of the processes and methods of scientific enquiry – this is essentially procedural understanding. The other three targets – Sc2, 3 and 4 are concerned with the 'content': – conceptual understanding. Although the Programmes of Study are separate, it would be difficult for them to develop separately. These are not the same as 'theory' and 'practical'; sometimes the aim of a practical activity will be conceptual understanding rather than procedural. There is also some 'theory' in procedural understanding in the basic model for scientific enquiry. It is clear that procedural understanding develops most effectively through certain types of practical work. The introduction of 'investigations' was seen as an important innovation in the National Curriculum proposals for science leading to procedural understanding. But there is a conceptual understanding dimension to Sc1 as well. For example, when pupils are developing hypotheses for their investigations they may well bring in their conceptual understanding on which to base a prediction that they will test – e.g. "I think that this material will be a good insulator because it has air trapped inside it and air is a poor conductor of heat."

Pupils may not recognise the relationship between these two sorts of understanding. This may be particularly true when they 'do a Sc1' where their concern may be confined to the procedural dimension. Failure to recognise the relationship between 'conceptual' and 'procedural' is likely to be made worse if the activity is not fully integrated within the topic but merely 'bolted-on'. There is a general concern (raised by writers such as Derek Hodson, Robin Millar and Brian Woolnough – see Bibliography p.97-98) over whether practical work in science is always as effective as it might be in developing either sort of understanding. Pupils often do not see how the practical work relates to the theory. Instead of helping them to see how science works and improving their understanding of the concepts, the practical work may actually confuse the message. Questions along the lines of "What's supposed to happen, Miss?" indicate this problem.

The use of IT simulations can act as effective extensions of, but not substitutes for, practical work. They allow considerable possibilities for the manipulation of variables in ways that real practicals may not. Furthermore, their limitations contain powerful teaching opportunities for pupils to begin to appreciate the procedural aspects of the investigations being modelled. In this way it can be shown how the conceptual knowledge derived is linked to the assumptions on which the model is based (Jon Scaife and Jerry Wellington discuss in detail the use of IT in learning science; see Bibliography, p.97-98).

Jerry Wellington suggests that ...

> *.. an insistence on practical work can actually restrict the science curriculum: 'We won't teach that topic because we can't do practical work with it.' This has led to an often hidden reluctance amongst science teachers to include a topic in a scheme of work because they cannot find a way of including a traditional practical.*

Secondary Science: Contemporary Issues and Practical Approaches,
J J Wellington (Routledge, 1994)

The Cognitive Acceleration through Science Education project (CASE) has an important part to play in helping children relate the conceptual and the procedural aspects of science through developing thinking skills that will bring them together. Focusing on areas such as variables and probability, the CASE project developed a series of simple thinking lessons for 12-13 year olds involving basic and inexpensive equipment. **'Thinking Science'** *(BP Educational Services)* is the set of materials written for the project. They encourage pupils to develop their thinking, in Piaget's terms, from the 'concrete operational' to the 'formal operational'.

Children at the formal operational level can deal with multi-variate problems and explain events rather than merely describe them. Formal operational thinking can be developed through exercises on:

- **control of variables, and exclusion of irrelevant variables**
- **ratio and proportionality**
- **compensation and equilibrium**
- **classification**
- **probability and correlation**
- **use of formal models to explain and predict**

OHT5

Examples of concrete and formal operational thinking

a) Jane planted some flowers in her garden. She measured one of them each week. Here is a graph of its height, which shows how well it grew.

■ When was the plant growing fastest?

■ What happened after June 20th?

To answer this question about plant growth straightforward one-to-one modelling using concrete operational thinking is required.

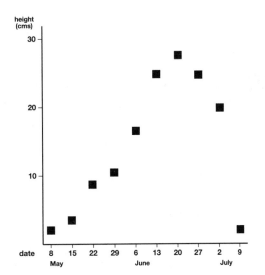

b) A lift can travel from the ground floor to the fifth floor of a building. It takes approximately 5 seconds to travel from one floor to the next. It stops for 10 seconds at each floor.

Which graph represents the movement of the lift?

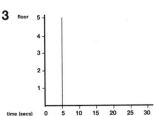

This question is more difficult because formal operational thinking is needed to process the variables of height (floor number) and time.

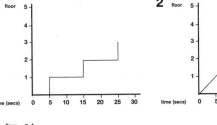

CASE

Effective Learning in Science

The key point for science teachers is that the project team has shown that real understanding of many of the concepts included in National Curriculum Programmes of Study for science require formal operational thinking. The CASE project demonstrates that the investment of time in teaching children how to *think* can have long-term benefits for their intellectual development. The claims from the project are far reaching – enhanced examination performance and transferability to other subject areas. Moreover, the teaching of thinking skills has the potential to promote the development of pupils' procedural knowledge whilst at the same time reinforcing their understanding of conceptual knowledge.

Integrating procedural and conceptual knowledge

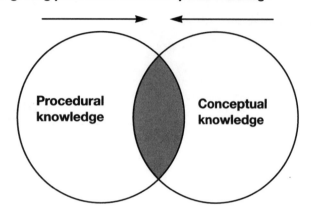

An appreciation of the relationship between procedural and conceptual knowledge promotes effective learning by offering learners opportunities to perform their understanding. Joseph Schwab wrote in the 1960s about 'substantive' and 'syntactic' knowledge – for us these are like the vocabulary and grammar of science. When learning a language, you cannot use either on its own with any real hope of communication – fluency only comes when the two are brought together. It is the same with procedural and conceptual scientific knowledge and understanding.

3 Learning preferences and styles

Effective learning probably means something different for all of us because we all learn in slightly different ways. Evidence here comes from a number of different sources but they are all sending the same message.

Some of us are 'serialists' and prefer to see the picture build up piece by piece; some of us are 'holists' and like to see the whole picture first in order to make sense of the individual parts.

A lot of work has been done with children and adults on learning styles. The work of David Kolb in the United States and Honey and Mumford in this country attempt through 'learning style inventories' to categorize different preferred styles of learning.

Using Kolb's analysis of learning styles as an example, how do you respond to these two questions?

- **Do you prefer real-life, tangible experiences or do you like to think about the ideas first?**
- **Do you like to be actively involved straightaway or do you like the opportunity to watch and reflect?**

The questions relate to two interrelated dimensions of our preferred learning style. Taking these as two continua, we can locate ourselves somewhere along these lines:

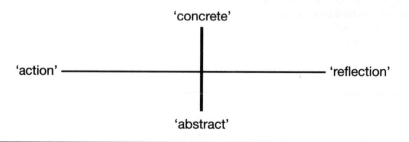

Superimposing these axes, we produce four learning style quadrants. The four desciptions below characterise typical groups of learners. Perhaps you recognise members of your classes?

Dynamic learners ...

- like to try things out and don't worry about getting it wrong
- enjoy variety and look for excitement
- are keen to take action and get others involved
- don't want to plan and don't want to check work
- manage their time badly

Common sense learners ...

- read instructions carefully and organise their time well
- enjoy solving problems by integrating theory and practice
- work well alone, are thorough and decisive
- like doing things their way but are not very imaginative
- want to get the job done but don't like being given answers

Imaginative learners ...

- like to see the whole picture and see relationships between ideas
- enjoy brainstorming sessions and using their imagination
- listen well and like group work
- work in fits and starts and forget important details
- are easily distracted and indecisive

Analytic learners ...

- are well organised and can work alone
- are analytical and logical and see links between ideas
- set clear goals and apply theories to problems
- don't like group discussion
- get bogged down in detail

OHT6

Each learning style has its good and its bad points. Kolb goes on to develop a model for what has become known as 'experiential learning' which incorporates episodes that will appeal to people of all four learning styles. He suggests that we need to recognise the strengths and weaknesses in our own preferred learning style and try to become more balanced learners whilst working through programmes which follow the sequence of the cycle.

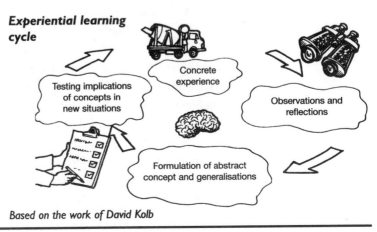

Experiential learning cycle

Concrete experience

Observations and reflections

Formulation of abstract concept and generalisations

Testing implications of concepts in new situations

Based on the work of David Kolb

There is a good account of Kolb's main ideas in Gordon Bell's **'Educating for Capability: A Practical Guide'** *(Royal Society of Arts, 1991)* along with a version of his learning styles inventory. The overall conclusion from this project is ...

> *.... that the capabilities of young people are best developed through a variety of teaching styles which promote different styles of learning.*

Kolb's analysis is not the only way we can think about approaches to learning. Research in Neuro-Linguistic Programming (NLP) suggests that there are three preferred 'modalities' which affect the way we use our senses to interpret our experiences. This is particularly important in relation to the way we conceptualise our learning goals.

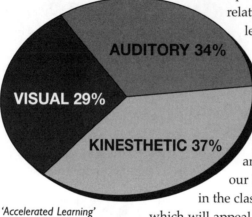

Learning modalities

AUDITORY 34%
VISUAL 29%
KINESTHETIC 37%

'Accelerated Learning'
A Smith (NEP)

Around 29% of us have a visual preference and want to *see* our goals; 34% of us have an auditory preference and will find language important – either spoken out loud or talking to ourselves; and 37% of us are kinesthetic and associate our learning with *'feelings'*. Thinking about this in the classroom, we can devise teaching approaches which will appeal to each type of learner.

- **Visual** – video, textbook, posters ...

- **Auditory** – discussion, speakers, question and answer sessions ...

- **Kinesthetic** – role plays, drama, practical activities ...

Harvard Professor Howard Gardner gives us insights into a rather different view on this by considering the concept of intelligence. He suggests that we have not one but seven sorts of intelligence and that the balance between them will vary from person to person. For Gardner, intelligence is not what is measured by 'IQ' tests but is an expandable set of competences in these areas which he sees as having distinctive features:

- linguistic
- mathematical and logical
- visual and spatial
- musical
- interpersonal
- intrapersonal
- kinesthetic

Most learners will have an uneven intelligence profile – being strong in some areas and relatively weak in others. The full implications of Gardner's theory of 'multiple intelligences' underpin ideas about 'Accelerated Learning' and are fully discussed in Alistair Smith's book of the same title in this series.

Smith also points to another learning preference – are you left-brained or right-brained? Left-brain activity is associated with serial processing – linearity, analysis, numbers, language. Right-brain activity is associated with parallel processing – patterns, images, pictures, relationships. These are sometimes stereotyped into left-brain – 'logical'; right-brain – 'creative' but the reality is much more complex. Although the brain integrates both forms of processing, we tend to favour one sort of activity over the other. We should be aiming for a 'whole-brain' approach to learning which provides both sorts of opportunities. Smith refers to the work of Bernice McCarthy who has built this into each of David Kolb's learning styles, giving an eight-stage cycle – the 4-MAT Cycle – which alternates phases favouring left- then right-brained activity.

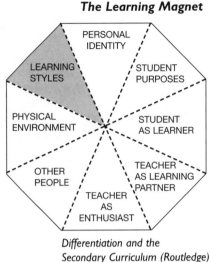

The Learning Magnet

*Differentiation and the
Secondary Curriculum (Routledge)*

Michael Fielding suggests that we should see learning styles as just one component of what he refers to as a 'human dimension of learning'. He represents this as a 'Learning Magnet' with eight elements, of which learning styles is just one sector.

There are several important questions for teachers in all of this. How aware are we of different learning styles and preferences? How are learning strategies which relate to these styles built into our teaching? Is there an unconscious relationship between our own preferred learning style and our preferred teaching style? If there is, then how will pupils respond?

4 Individual differences

The match between the activities which students are given in the school and their needs is the subject of comment from many school inspections. In reports these 'needs' are usually associated with students' abilities:

> *In order to provide effective teaching for pupils of all abilities, teachers should consider whether:*
>
> ● *the teaching method adopted ... is the best to give pupils of all abilities, including those with special educational needs, the maximum chance to make progress;*
>
> ● *the materials used and the tasks set are designed so that all pupils are appropriately challenged but can respond to them at a range of levels.*
>
> *In order to raise standards of scientific knowledge and understanding, teachers need to give greater attention to matching their teaching to the attainment and ability of the class and to ensuring that pupils build a coherent framework of scientific ideas.*

Subjects and Standards *(HMSO, 1996)*

We have already seen that when we think of differences in 'needs' we should take into account the influence of prior experience, learning preferences as well as differences in attainment and ability. There are many other differences which can have a significant influence on learning. We consider briefly in Section Two how gender, and racial and cultural differences may have an influence on the shape of the curriculum and the way we teach it. If these differences are ignored individuals may not feel valued. This can have quite a fundamental effect on learning itself and particularly on their motivation to learn.

Responding to individual needs – an evolutionary process?

Responding to individual needs has been a central concern in teaching since the introduction of mixed-ability grouping in the 1960s and 70s. One response to the 'problem' of teaching mixed ability groups was the development of 'resource-based' and 'individualised learning' schemes, introduced as an alternative to class teaching which was seen as inappropriate for a range of abilities. Later developments building on these foundations were seen in approaches such as 'flexible' and 'open learning' and 'supported self-study' where learning programmes were designed on a more individual basis encouraging learners to take more responsibility for their learning. There were elements of this in use of the term 'active learning' in the 1980s where the emphasis was clearly on the learner's role in the learning process. At the start of this sequence of innovations 'individual needs' may have been seen principally in terms of ability and attainment but other sorts of need, as discussed above, have undoubtedly become incorporated into developments in more recent years.

In the 1990s this issue is often set within the context of 'differentiation'. A simple definition of differentiation is ...

... the organisation of teaching and learning to meet individual needs.

An obvious way of doing this might be by identifying needs and grouping pupils accordingly. Bob Stradling and Lesley Saunders, writing about the NFER Lower Attaining Pupils Programme, do not believe that meeting individual needs can be achieved through grouping strategies such as setting or banding which tend to focus on one aspect of individual needs – that is, differences in ability:

> *Strategies for differentiation need to be framed in terms of its purpose, which is to maximise the motivation, progress and achievement of each student. In other words, differentiation should be thought of a pedagogical rather than an organisational strategy. It is the process of matching learning targets, tasks, activities, resources and learning support to individual learners' needs, styles and rates of learning.*

Differentiation in practice *(Educational Research, 35 [2], 1993)*

There are several possible approaches to differentiation but a useful framework is offered by Chris Dickinson and Julie Wright in the book **'Differentiation: a practical handbook of classroom strategies'** *(NCET, 1993)*. This model has been further developed in Chris Dickinson's book **'Effective Learning Activities'** in this series.

Dickinson's model, shown on the opposite page, offers a more sophisticated approach than the common distinction between 'differentiation by task' and 'differentiation by outcome'. Here we can see that differentiation can not only be achieved through thinking about the tasks or activities to which pupils are directed but also through use of a variety of resources. Tasks and activities will generate outcomes but it is through the support given to pupils whilst working on the tasks and the response given to them that further differentiation will be possible.

Another model comes from work by the Northamptonshire Inspection and Advisory Service Science Team which proposes a differentiation cycle, shown below.

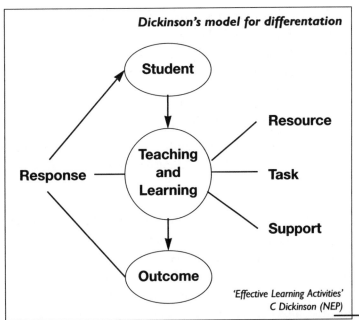

Dickinson's model for differentiation

'Effective Learning Activities'
C Dickinson (NEP)

OHT7

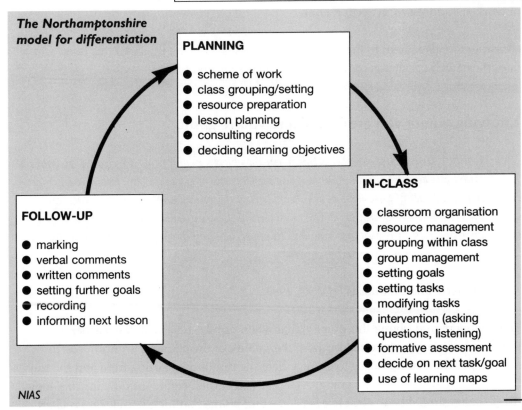

The Northamptonshire model for differentiation

PLANNING

- scheme of work
- class grouping/setting
- resource preparation
- lesson planning
- consulting records
- deciding learning objectives

IN-CLASS

- classroom organisation
- resource management
- grouping within class
- group management
- setting goals
- setting tasks
- modifying tasks
- intervention (asking questions, listening)
- formative assessment
- decide on next task/goal
- use of learning maps

FOLLOW-UP

- marking
- verbal comments
- written comments
- setting further goals
- recording
- informing next lesson

NIAS

OHT8

In both these models 'differentiation by outcome' becomes a rather redundant idea other than in terms of assessment. In fact the NIAS Science Team refer to it as 'differentiation by accident'!

All these developments from the 1960s to the 1990s have presented a challenge to the stereotypical class lesson with the teacher at the front of the class and pupils working mainly on the same activity. The furthest we may be prepared to go is to recognise that pupils will work at different rates if we give them, for example, a worksheet-based activity, and that we may need some extension work if the quickest (and often assumed the 'brightest') finish early.

And yet, there is a strong sense in which, if we are going to respond to pupils' learning needs (and not just in terms of ability), we will need to think of pupils working on different activities at the same time for an increased proportion of lessons. This will not only require new classroom management strategies, but it will need some organising framework on which to base decisions about what pupils need to cover. If we are following an agreed curriculum as we are in all parts of the UK, then in one sense, everyone has to cover the same content. But do they need to cover it in the same depth or in the same way?

Currently most schemes of work, particularly for the 11-14 age range, seem to suggest they do. There is some differentiation of content through the 'tiering' arrangements in GCSE syllabuses but little guidance even here about progression of ideas within the tiers.

There is a close link between the extent to which the curriculum can be differentiated and the structure of the scheme of work we are using to translate our programmes of study into operational terms. We need to have more sophisticated schemes of work which analyse the content, and indicate possible routes through it, that will respond to learners' needs and provide us with a clear view about the progression of ideas and relationships between them. Possible approaches to the development of such a scheme of work are addressed in Section Four.

Classroom management to meet individual needs is a central theme of this book and underlies much of what is contained in Sections Five and Six.

5 Knowing where you are and where you're going

> *Teaching is seen to be more effective when the objectives of lessons are clear. This requires sound overall curriculum planning, so that teachers in turn can plan and prepare coherent series of lessons in which they identify the progress in knowledge, skills and understanding to be achieved. The more clearly these expected outcomes are identified, the more likely it is also that they will be appreciated by the pupils, so that both share a greater sense of purpose and progress.*

Subjects and Standards *(HMSO, 1996)*

The argument underlying this point is that when pupils share with the teacher a common and clearly identified purpose the quality of the learning is improved. To achieve this the teacher needs to know where the pupils are starting from and the pupils need to know where they are going. As suggested earlier, before introducing any topic the first step should be to elicit learners' starting points and identify relevant related knowledge already encountered. This sounds obvious but OFSTED report that this is often missing:

> *.. Other common weaknesses are a failure to give sufficient attention to consolidating learning or to linking current work with that covered previously.*

Subjects and Standards *(HMSO, 1996)*

The implication of the above is that there are occasions when pupils do not have a clear sense of purpose. When asked about why they are undertaking a particular piece of work, theoretical or practical, they are most likely to respond in a way that suggests they are simply following instructions.

The view being presented here is that there is merit in the learning objectives being revealed in such a way that pupils are enabled to share in the purposes of their work and to have a perspective about where it is leading. Indeed, knowing the criteria for success is crucial if pupils are going to:

- **understand what is meant by success**
  and . . .
- **recognise how they can improve.**

To reinforce this, the OFSTED Handbook confirms that this is what inspectors will be looking for as they are required to judge whether:

> *.. pupils are clear about what they are doing, why they are doing it, how long they have to do it and the way in which they can judge success in their work.*

Guidance on the Inspection of Secondary Schools *(HMSO, 1995)*

Many pupils at work in the science laboratory are usually able to explain what they are doing, but how many are able to say why? Is effective learning likely to be taking place if they cannot answer the 'why?' question? If they cannot answer the question 'why?' how can they possibly go on to judge success in their work?

An approach involving pupils in this way has implications for assessment. In the first place it is likely that formative asessment, and diagnostic testing within that, will have an important role to play. Curriculum planning will naturally build the assessment into the learning process and lead to a clearer statement of criteria or targets for success. Any criterion referenced system of assessment such as this depends crucially on the principle of making targets explicit to the pupils before the teaching begins.

Mastery learning, for example, is based on this principle. Learning objectives are made clear to the pupils at the outset and diagnostic tests based on those objectives are employed to check for the conceptual/procedural problems pupils experience with the subject matter. This approach is discussed fully in Keith Postlethwaite's book **'Differentiated Science Teaching'** *(Open University Press, 1993).*

An approach to curriculum planning as suggested in Section Four, involving concept mapping or any other comparable approach, would help to ensure that appropriate links are forged with related content areas or over-arching principles. Identifying conceptual progression will increase the probability of effective consolidation.

6 Building motivation and ownership

Most teachers would agree that there is a close link between motivation and effective learning. The American psychologist Abraham Maslow, in his book **'Motivation and Personality,** *(Harper Row, 1970),* suggested a model for motivation (shown on the right) which relates to a hierarchy of basic human needs.

Maslow suggests that we pay greatest attention to the lowest level in the hierarchy which is not currently being satisfied at that time. This particularly applies to children and adolescents but adults may also respond in this way. Thus, if it is approaching lunch break, children

Maslow's heirarchy of needs

Fulfilling one's potential

Self-esteem

Emotional needs (affection/'belonging')

Safety (physical and psychological)

Physiological needs (food, shelter, etc.)

are unlikely to be concerned with fulfilling their potential but rather with filling their stomachs! More seriously, if children do not feel secure in the classroom because learning creates stress rather than challenge, are they likely to be effective learners? Attending to all levels in the hierarchy below the top one is going to be important in maintaining motivation for meaningful learning.

There is also a hierarchy of cognitive levels (see Section Four) which interconnect and to some extent correlate with this hierarchy of basic needs. Thus, children may need information in order for them to feel safe. The relationship between motivation and learning is further discussed in Keith Postlethwaite's book **'Differentiated Science Teaching'** *(Open University Press, 1993)*.

There is a link here with what we know about blood flow in the brain (see Alastair Smith's book **'Accelerated Learning'** in this series). In stressful situations 'flight-or-fight' responses tend to direct blood towards areas of the brain concerned with physical response and away from those areas concerned with higher level processing. Learning in these conditions may be very limited and superficial.

This aspect of effective learning is also related to the previous area. Without an understanding of purpose, pupils are unlikely to be motivated or feel any sense of ownership of the activity. Research shows that in many instances the teacher's purpose for setting an activity does not match the purpose of the pupils who are doing it. Osborne and Freyburg indicate that this has various consequences:

> - *Some pupils who cannot immediately perceive a purpose for a lesson limit themselves to low level intellectual involvement and follow the instructions.*
> - *Some pupils establish their alternative purposes which the teacher may not realise.*
> - *Some pupils who do not recognise the purpose, instead recognise they need to get the 'right answer'.*
> - *Some teachers establish purposes for a lesson which are not shared with the pupils, and which are frequently not achieved.*

Learning in Science, *R Osborne & P Freyburg (Heinemann, 1985)*

A criticism of providing the pupils with objectives or criteria which make it clear where they are going is that it is the same as telling them the answer – it removes opportunity for strategic surprises. Many teachers wish to use strategies where certain kinds of discovery or surprises occur. This is to be encouraged and is not a contradiction with sharing success criteria with the pupils.

Sharing sufficient information concerning 'purpose' with pupils so that they can see where they are going is a motivational strategy designed to engender ownership. Where there is a strong sense of ownership you are more likely to engender intrinsic motivation. In turn, where pupils are motivated intrinsically there is a greater chance they will be able to take more responsibility for their own learning.

Here is a simple example:

> Carrying out food tests is a common practical exercise. Normally pupils are asked to identify the presence or absence of protein, starch, fat, etc., in a range of familiar foods. What is the purpose of this activity? What is the intrinsic motivation for them to want to find out what's in the food?

Children hold a lot of knowledge (some of it scientifically incorrect) about what is in food. Setting a relevant context for an inquiry, (e.g. identifying a diet for a diabetic, designing a low-fat, high-protein diet, etc.) is essential for stimulating curiosity. Asking pupils to share knowledge to predict levels of protein/fat/carbohydrate in particular foods before carrying out any tests and to review their predictions in the light of the outcomes has a better chance of engendering intrinsic motivation than following a 'recipe'. The end point for success is clear.

In this way the pupil-perceived purpose for a task and the teacher-perceived purpose for the task coincide.

7 Valuing prior learning

The science curriculum in all parts of the UK is designed to offer children the opportunity to experience a science education which provides continuity and progression between, as well as within, phases. Recent research shows that the experiences in science that pupils bring with them when they cross phase from primary to secondary school is very variable and depends crucially on the nature of the science teaching they received. Teachers in the primary phase with a limited science background may tend to offer pupils a body or list of unrelated facts, whereas specialist science teachers are more likely to provide a more coherent framework.

The view still persists amongst secondary school science teachers that this creates an insurmountable problem to which the only solution is to wipe the slate clean so that each incoming group of Year 7 pupils can have a common starting point. Unfortunately this ignores all we have gathered from the research into children's learning in science. We ignore prior knowledge at our peril as we know it influences subsequent learning.

> *Children from a young age, and prior to learning science at school, have meanings for words and views of the world which are to them sensible and useful. Such views can be strongly held and are often not recognised by teachers, but nevertheless influence the formal learning of science in many unintended ways.*

Learning in Science, *R Osborne & P Freyburg (Heinemann, 1985)*

The clean slate approach also rejects the proposition that some children will enter secondary school with a relatively high level of knowledge and understanding. The point made strongly by school inspectors is that progress depends on teachers' expectations and that where teachers do not expect enough of their pupils the pace of learning suffers and pupils lose motivation. With regard to the phase transition between the primary and secondary school OFSTED reports that:

> *This problem is particularly acute in the first years of secondary school, where an often indiscriminate assumption of the need to make a 'fresh start' ignores the level of attainment reached and the learning skills acquired by the pupils in the primary school. This causes many to mark time at the start of their secondary course instead of launching into more challenging work.*

Subject and Standards *(HMSO, 1996)*

It advocates that greater attention needs to be paid to children's primary school experience and that teaching should be matched to pupils' different levels of attainment.

Most children are willing to learn and their positive attitudes at that age can best be harnessed and translated into learning if the intellectual stimulus is sufficiently challenging.

Two major points emerge:

- **All pupils come to secondary school with ideas about science which will influence their learning and should therefore be recognised.**

- **Some pupils will come with a good knowledge base in science which should be valued.**

If effective learning is to take place teaching approaches ought to acknowledge what children already know. To achieve this the science teacher must be able to transform the subject matter in ways which will both build on pupils' prior knowledge as well as diagnose lack of knowledge and misconceptions. The implications for planning are obvious if pupils are to avoid spending excessive amounts of time on activities which do not contribute to their knowledge, skills or understanding.

School inspections

In all the areas considered so far there is some sort of research evidence or 'theory' to support what has been advanced as influencing our thinking about effective learning. It is not always clear where the theoretical roots of some of the statements issuing from government are located but it will be of importance to consider what sorts of indicators school inspectors use to judge effective learning. Many of these are linked to relative standards of performance as measured through national testing. In addition the inspection framework also looks at the quality of learning in the classroom using other indicators which reflect the pupils' **attitude** to learning. Quality is seen in the following terms:

Do pupils show interest in their work? Are they able to sustain concentration and extend their capacity for personal study?

Inspectors should look for evidence of pupils' involvement in and enjoyment of learning, their willingness to apply themselves to the task in hand, respond to challenging tasks, to learn from mistakes, to ask and answer questions, to join in discussion and show enthusiasm.

Important evidence should emerge from discussion with pupils about whether they enjoy their work, what they find easy or difficult; how they tackle new work and what they think of their contributions in lessons.

A positive approach to work is shown in:
- *their concentration in listening to the teacher;*
- *how confidently pupils work independently to generate ideas and solve problems;*
- *their capacity to persevere and complete tasks when difficulties arise;*
- *their ability to select and use relevant resources;*
- *their desire to improve their work and their pride in the finished product.*

There should be evidence of older pupils and students carrying more responsibility for the organisation of their work, taking the initiative and setting some of their own tasks in discussion with their teachers.

Guidance on the Inspection of Secondary Schools *(HMSO, 1995)*

The key elements here seem to be to do with pupils' interest and motivation, engagement with the task, a clear idea of why they are doing it and some element (with older children at least) of taking some responsibility for their own learning. These ideas would seem to be in line with many of the points made earlier and may strengthen the case for greater attention being paid to them whether or not an inspection is looming!

Where next?

We could have written a whole book on each of the issues discussed in this section. Indeed many books have been written and we have referred to some of them in the discussion. Our aim has been to recognise that there are a number of different, but in many ways related, ideas about what characterises effective learning. To conclude this section we would like to summarise these as a set of criteria against which to evaluate current and future practice. We will return to these points throughout the rest of the book and particularly in Section Three where we will encourage you to consider how they relate to your school situation.

These statements can be taken as a set on principles for good practice. In this section we have suggested that learning is more likely to be effective if ...

- ... there are opportunities to build on children's own ideas

- ... there is a clear relationship between procedural and conceptual understanding

- ... teaching approaches recognise that pupils learn in different ways

- ... activities are related to pupils' needs

- ... pupils 'know where they are going'

- ... pupils are given appropriate challenges

- ... pupils are well motivated and have positive attitudes

- ... prior learning is recognised and valued

OHT9

Section Two

What sort of science? What sort of science teachers?

In Section One we considered the question of effective learning from the learners' viewpoint, but recognised that we would also need to relate this to the content of what we as science teachers are required to teach them and want them to learn. In this section we would like to think about:

- **the content and process of the current science curriculum**
- **the possible future shaping of the science curriculum as we move into the next century**
- **the sort of knowledge that will be important for science teachers in the 21st Century**

The science curriculum – content and process?

The introduction of the National Curriculum in England and Wales in 1989 put into place a common national framework for what science should be taught in schools. The statutory part defined the content ('what') fairly clearly through Programmes of Study but said little about 'why' students should study science. In order to provide some insights into this the government advisory bodies in place at the time (the National Curriculum Council and the Curriculum Council for Wales) produced Non-Statutory Guidance. In both versions, a number of ways are outlined in which science can make a contribution to a pupil's education. These are from the CCW:

- *Development of pupils' ability to use scientific methods of investigation*

- *Development of understanding of scientific ideas*

- *Cultivation of positive personal qualities and attitudes*

- *Development of critical awareness of the role of science in society*

- *Development of a balanced appreciation of the power and the limitations of science as a human activity*

- *Access to a wide range of careers*

Non-Statutory Guidance for Science *(CCW, 1989)*

The last of these is more of an entitlement that comes from studying science rather than an aim or goal in terms of learning. The first two objectives are clearly evident in the programmes of study for the National Curriculum which define the attainment targets for science: the first relating to 'Science 1 – Experimental and Investigative Science' (Sc1); and the second relating to the 'content' attainment targets 'Sc2 – Life Processes and Living Things', 'Sc3 – Materials and their Properties' and 'Sc4 – Physical Processes'.

But ...

> ... where are the third, fourth and fifth objectives in the programmes of study?

> ... how are they represented in your schemes of work?

> ... how do you address them in the classroom?

With the revisions of the National Curriculum in 1992 and 1995 these areas have become more and more obscure (particularly with the removal of the old 'AT17 – the Nature of Science'). The emphasis has become increasingly focused on simply defining the 'knowledge-base' for school science. It is true that there is a general introduction to the programmes of study (sometimes referred to as 'Sc0') which does include reference to these areas and it is of course still possible for teachers to bring them into their teaching. However, when the statutory part emphasises a factual content, and this is the focus for the national testing both through Key Stage 3 tests and GCSEs, it is not suprising that these elements have often been seen as less important, marginalised or forgotten altogether!

When we think about effective learning in science we would argue that is important to think not only about how we are teaching (which was the main concern in Section One) but also about what we are teaching and why we are teaching it.

Science curriculum for the 21st Century

If we look towards Scotland, we find that a more reflective approach to changing the curriculum has been adopted than south of the border. The Scottish Consultative Council on the Curriculum (SCCC) began reviewing science education in Scottish Schools in 1992. In a recent consultation and discussion paper, James Graham, Chair of the Science Review Group states that ...

> *.. it will, we believe, be most important that those involved resist the temptation to rush into highly detailed analysis of implications for curricula and resources at this time. Instead, we regard it as essential, as we move towards the new millenium, that all those with an interest in science education should take time to ponder matters which are fundamental to its continued relevance and value for all our young people. We have, perhaps, rushed ahead too often and too quickly in this and other areas of the curriculum in the past.*

Science Education for Scottish Schools (SCCC, 1996)

In view of the very hurried introduction of the National Curriculum in England and Wales, it is perhaps reassuring to hear that Scotland will take a more measured approach to reshaping the curriculum. In the United States, the time scale is even longer; Project 2061 looks forward to the year in which Halley's Comet is due to return as its target date!

A major factor influencing the initiation of the review in Scotland was the ...

> *.. awareness of both the power and limitations of science as a prominent feature of contemporary Scottish society and the consequent and growing importance of a more 'scientifically literate' citizenry in the years ahead.*

Science Education for Scottish Schools (SCCC, 1996)

There is nothing to suggest that this idea does not also apply equally in England and Wales the and indeed the notion of 'scientific literacy' underlies the public understanding of the science movement which has widespread support both in goverment and the scientific community. The Committee for the Public Understanding of Science (COPUS) is a high-status body involving the Royal Society, the Royal Institution and the British Association for the Advancement of Science. The aims of COPUS for science in schools are reflected in the following quote:

> *For individual learners, experience of science education should:*
>
> - *Broaden understanding of themselves, human cultures and societies and the natural and made worlds in which they live.*
> - *Help to sustain natural human curiosity, develop an enquiring mind and foster an interest in continuing to learn throughout life.*
> - *Help to engender a critical way of thinking about phenomena and issues.*
> - *Support other aspects of learning across the curriculum.*
> - *Develop the potential to contribute in an informed, thoughtful and sensitive way to the enhancement of people's lives and of the environment.*

Science Education for Scottish Schools *(SCCC, 1996)*

It is interesting to see that the emphasis here is not on science as a body of knowledge or even a process of enquiry, but on developing what the paper refers to as 'scientific capability'. There would obviously need to be some knowledge base but this would be selected in relation to these broader aims. The view is very much looking forward:

> *Young people face a future dominated by change. A major aim of education should be to help them understand the interconnections between various types of change so that they can respond thoughtfully, critically, sensitively and constructively. ... the provision of an appropriate and effective education in science for every young person is likely to become ever more important for the health and prosperity of society and the future well-being of the planet.*

Science Education for Scottish Schools *(SCCC, 1996)*

This sort of statement takes us away from the constraints imposed by the content-dominated National Curriculum in English and Welsh schools towards the difficult task of trying to predict what an appropriate science curriculum would look like for children moving into the next century.

Crystal ball gazing can be an uncertain and even dangerous practice but the information revolution might suggest that acquisition of factual knowledge may be overtaken by the skills needed to access it, and that depth of understanding of key ideas might be more important than a superficial grasp of a broad range of topics.

The RSA Educating for Capability in Schools Project (see Section One) was intended to help people become more effective as well as knowledgeable. Education for capability aims to encourage and develop four capacities (the '4 Cs'), listed over the page.

Effective Learning in Science

33

Competence *can be improved through the practice of skills and through the application of knowledge.*

Coping skills *can be developed through experience of handling problems facing one's self and society.*

Creativity *can be promoted through tackling open-ended as opposed to closed problems.*

Co-operation *can be developed through experience of working in teams.*

An important dimension of developing capability is giving young people greater responsibility for their own learning.

OHT10

Educating for Capability: A Practical Guide, *G Bell (RSA, 1991)*

It is clear that science can and should be making a major contribution to the development of these capacities. Guy Claxton's ideas about effective schooling are also useful in emphasising the development of thinking skills and problem-solving approaches for which science can provide many opportunities. Claxton suggests that we have three sorts of intelligence:

- the first sort is the traditional concept to do with the amount of knowledge we have – knowing *that*;

- the second sort is about using our knowledge and skills so that we know what to do in particular situations – knowing *how*;

- and the third sort is, as Claxton puts it – 'knowing what to do when you don't know what to do'!

OHT11

This third intelligence is perhaps a way of helping us find a way forward in preparing pupils for 'a future dominated by change'. In an article entitled 'A 2020 Vision of Education' in **'Science Today: Problem or Crisis'** edited by R Levinson and J Thomas, *(Routledge 1997)*, Claxton argues that the qualities we need to be encouraging children to develop are his new '3Rs' – Resilience, Resourcefulness and Reflection – to go with Bell's '4Cs' (see above). These emphasise learners being flexible, learning from their mistakes, thinking about their learning and having strategies to cope with new situations. This view has obvious relevance to science education and again takes us away from seeing the subject as a body of knowledge and much more towards stressing the process of enquiry. When we read of 'scientific capability', is this what we mean?

In their discussion paper, the SCCC develop the notion of 'scientific capability' (to use in preference to 'scientific literacy') "because it conveys more clearly a flavour of science education for *action* as well as for personal enlightenment and satisfaction".

Scientific capability is seen as having five aspects which could help in thinking about what we are trying to achieve in science education in schools:

- An enquiring habit of mind – *scientific curiosity*
- Ability to investigate scientifically – *scientific competence*
- Understanding of scientific ideas and the way science works – *scientific understanding*
- Ability to think and act creatively – *scientific creativity*
- Critical awareness of the role of science in society combined with a caring and responsible disposition – *scientific sensitivity*

OHT12

Science Education for Scottish Schools *(SCCC, 1996)*

There are clear links with some aspects of the National Curriculum but there are no programmes of study for scientific curiosity or sensitivity. These may develop but the chances will depend on the way we approach our teaching.

There does need to be a knowledge base for scientific understanding and competence but we need to remember the other aspects of scientific capability if our students are to have a 'balanced' science education. We also need to remember some of the points made in Section One about other 'balances' which have an influence on the content of the curriculum – between procedural and conceptual knowledge or between children's ideas of science and the accepted scientific viewpoint.

Research into gender issues in science in the 1980s showed how girls are often 'turned off' science during secondary schooling. It may be that they are treated differently from boys in the classroom – girls are asked questions less frequently – boys rush to the front to collect equipment. But there are also more subtle influences. In discussing scientific discoveries, how many women scientists are recognised? How is 'real science' portrayed through the textbooks and resources we use? – Impersonal? – Male dominated? How many women science teachers are there in the department? How many hold posts of responsibility?

Imbalances here can reinforce an image of the subject which presents science as lacking a human, caring side which can alienate some children – perhaps some boys as well as girls. There are some similar concerns regarding ethnic differences. Again, is science seen from a predominantly Western European/North American standpoint? What sort of messages does this give to both black children and white children? The debate about these aspects of equal opportunities in education range from the 'liberal' (girl-friendly/multicultural science) to what can be a highly political stance (feminist/anti-racist science). We do not intend to deal with these issues in detail here. A very thoughtful and constructive account of the issues themselves, along with many ideas for broadening science teaching to incorporate these perspectives, is contained in Michael Reiss's book **'Science Education for a Pluralist Society'** *(Open University Press, 1993)*. Again, there are implications both for the content of the curriculum and for the way science is taught.

Presenting children with the ways in which our present day science knowledge has been developed can be a potentially rich approach. This provides a way of bringing in the human dimension which may well appeal to girls by showing some relevance and at the same time introducing historical and cultural dimensions. The stories of people and science have the potential to capture children's imagination. Take for instance, the circulation of the blood:

- What contribution did Chinese, Greek and Islamic scientists make to the understanding of circulation?
- Was William Harvey aware of any of these when he studied it?
- What was the historical/religious context for Harvey's work?
- What other knowledge about the human body existed which guided experimentation at the time?
- How did Harvey go about it?
- Why did he have to be so painstaking in his explanations?
- What was the 'missing link' to complete Harvey's theory?
- When was that link made and by whom?

The ideas in **'Exploring the Nature of Science at Key Stage 3'**, *Joan Solomon (Blackie, 1991)* and **'Exploring the Nature of Science at Key Stage 4'**, *Solomon, Duveen & Scott (ASE, 1991)* are rich with ideas to help pupils see how experiments and the growth of knowledge in science are related.

This question of context and relevance is a major theme in Brian Woolnough's book **'Effective Science Teaching'** *(Open University Press, 1994)*, in which he argues for much more emphasis on students working on extended research projects. These are based on problems of real concern to the students which provide them with challenges and stimuli to develop both knowledge and creativity. He also stresses the importance of 'extra-curricular science' in enthusing children with a view of science as lively and sociable rather than the cold, fragmented, impersonal experience many children associate with the subject. Examples are:

- Science Clubs
- Involvement with BA Young Investigators or the CREST award scheme
- Science competitions
- Visits to interactive/hands-on science centres
- Developing links with industry

The knowledge base may be to some extent prescribed for us through our own national curricula but this should not cause us to forget why we want children to learn science. We still have some flexibility in the way we teach our subject and we should use this to move us towards a more appropriate curriculum for the next century.

Science teachers for the 21st Century

Undoubtedly, [good science teachers] are the key to effective science teaching, both in determining and delivering the curriculum, and in their relationships with the students in and out of class. For many scientists, engineers and medics, the most influential factor determining their career choice was an inspirational science teacher. For many who did not follow science into a career beyond school, their enjoyment and appreciation of science was also determined by their science teacher.

Effective Science Teaching, *B E Woolnough (Open University Press, 1994)*

There is a widely-held belief that all you need to be a teacher is a good knowledge of your subject. Our personal knowledge about subject matter is built up in a number of ways through our formal and informal experiences and is very important – but there is a

Modelling electrical circuits

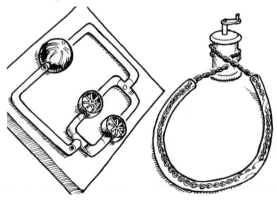

Conventional model   Solomon's model

difference between personal knowledge and the sort of knowledge needed for representing that subject matter in a way that is accessible to a group of learners. This sort of knowledge not only includes forms of representation of scientific phenomena such as metaphors, analogies, models, anecdotes, illustrations, historical perspectives or activities, but also recognises their strengths and weaknesses as representations of those phenomena.

For example, when we use a model with tubes and pumps to discuss electricity and electrical circuits, are we clear about the ways in which this is a good representation? What are its limitations? Joan Solomon (University of Oxford) uses a model with a length of bath-plug chain wound round a cotton reel. In what ways is this a better model? When we say this model is 'like' an electrical circuit, what do we mean by 'like' and how do our pupils interpret that word? Does 'like' mean 'just the same as' or does it mean 'similar to, in some ways'?

The sort of knowledge we are talking about here helps you to choose appropriately from a range of mental resources when planning lessons or during lessons themselves, or when developing teaching materials. It is also the sort of knowledge that can produce 'stories' of science which can interest pupils by providing the human dimension; that can encourage imagination and arouse curiosity; that can provide the right question at the right point to explain, to stimulate and to challenge. The quality of teachers' explanations was a recurring feature in a Scottish study of differentiation practice – **'What's the difference?'**, *M Simpson & J Ure (Northern College, 1993)*. A full treatment of the importance of this is contained in **'Explaining Science in the Classroom'** by Jon Ogborn and others *(Open University Press, 1996)*.

This knowledge is much more than a few 'tips for teachers'! It takes time and motivation to acquire but is very important for effective teaching. It is a specialised form of teachers' professional knowledge and comes from an integration between our personal knowledge of the subject and our knowledge about teaching and learning – pedagogy.

Lee Shulman, an American researcher, identified this form of teachers' knowledge and called it 'pedagogical content knowledge' (PCK). He describes it as that highly specialised form of knowledge acquired over time that derives specifically from the combination of an experienced science teacher's profound understanding of the subject matter and his/her knowledge of the learners. It involves strategies and other pedagogical techniques which the teacher uses to manipulate and transform the content into forms understandable to the learners in question.

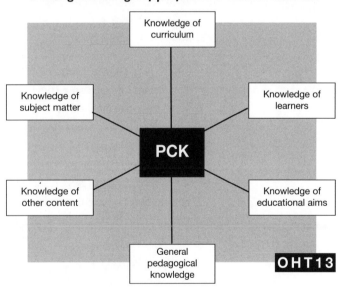

Pedagogical Content Knowledge – the craft and working knowledge of professional science teachers

Adapted from 'Exploring teachers' thinking', J Calderhead (Cassell Educational, 1987) p.113

The introduction of balanced science in the 1980s undoubtedly increased pupils' access and entitlement to the subject but was not always implemented in a way that addressed the associated professional development needs of the teachers. In those schools which introduced integrated or modular approaches, many teachers found themselves teaching outside their main science subject specialism with minimal additional professional training to help develop their own personal knowledge let alone 'PCK'.

To cope with this problem most departments aim to provide guidance through prescriptive schemes of work which list what is required to be taught often in a rigid lesson-by-lesson format. Although these schemes of work are meant to be helpful, especially to the non-specialist teacher, they do not necessarily provide detail about the knowledge and skills underpinning the representations that effective specialist teachers use to bring life and relevance to their teaching.

There have been some lost opportunities for collaboration in the development of schemes of work. Because of the very short time available to produce these before implementation, a common approach has been to send off the specialist physicist to produce the 'physics bits', the biologist to produce the 'biology bits', and so on. The preclusions of such collaboration, however, will further reduce opportunities for teachers to share and develop the professional knowledge base for science teaching that Professor Rosalind Driver, for example, called for in a paper entitled 'What is the use of theory in science teaching?' (given at the ASE INSET Services 1996 Annual Conference on Quality in Science Teaching). Within that professional knowledge base she stressed pedagogical content knowledge as being that innovative form of the science teacher's special knowledge which allows the content to be transformed in ways that make it accessible to all the pupils.

We argue that the need for the acquisition of pedagogical content knowledge makes the case for a collaborative model of curriculum planning and development even more compelling.

A collaborative model has the potential to promote a powerful way forward for any science department wishing to develop effective teaching and learning and encourage forward-looking professional development among its members. In Section Four, we suggest an approach to developing schemes of work which can exploit the advantages of collaborative planning and provide opportunities for members of the department to share their PCK. We believe that PCK is a helpful and useful concept that describes a kind of knowledge needed by all science teachers, whether teaching in their subject specialism or not. It involves knowledge about the kinds of misconceptions and alternative ideas that pupils bring with them to science lessons; about the range of strategies and activities which can be employed to identify and remedy them; and about the relationship between procedural and conceptual understanding.

There is a clear link here to the characteristics of effective learning which we identified in Section One. Even experienced teachers might be hard-pressed to identify in detail how they developed their PCK. It is something that is gradually acquired over time, from colleagues, from reading around the subject, from a range of other professional activities. It is part of the craft skills which are passed on within science departments and between teachers working together on developing their teaching. Your colleagues are a major resource; a good Head of Science will look for ways to exploit this – to divine their expertise and create ways of sharing it. It is not clear if PCK is 'taught or caught'; perhaps the best we can do is to look for ways of expediting its development.

REVIEW OF SECTION TWO

- The National Curriculum and examinations apart, can you identify other influences that currently shape the science curriculum you offer?

- In a changing world, what is the vision your science department holds for science education in the future?

- What meaning do the concepts of scientific literacy and capability have for your department and for pupils' learning?

- What opportunities are there for the imagination and creativity of both teachers and pupils to be harnessed in the evolution of the science curriculum?

- If science teaching should have a well-defined and clearly articulated knowledge base how is it expressed and shared in your department?

Providing a science education ———————————————— 2.1

Purpose:
The purpose of this activity is to review the over-arching purposes of the science education being provided.

Activity:
The activity offers a sample range of questions designed to get you to think beyond coverage of the content outlined in the National Curriculum and to ask how you think you will be meeting your pupils' needs for the next millenium.

1   Read pages 33-35 about what sort of science education various sources are encouraging us to provide as we move into the next century.

2   Identify the target group pupils.

3   Use the questions and follow-up activities to review the purposes of your science department.

   a)   Do you prepare your pupils to be scientifically literate?
        Agree on a set of criteria which could be used to identify a pupil as being scientifically literate.
        Identify the activities which provide genuine opportunities to meet these criteria.

   b)   Do you expect pupils to demonstrate scientific capability?
        Agree on a set of criteria which could be used as indicative of scientific capability.
        Design an activity requiring pupils to employ scientific reasoning as a means of evaluating your claims.

   c)   Do you aim to foster a spirit of imagination and creativity?
        Identify the opportunities pupils have to develop such attitudes.
        Design a simple questionnaire to assess the development of pupils' predisposition to apply their scientific knowledge to unfamiliar situations.

Notes:
Section Two introduces a range of sources which you might use as a basis to reassess the current policy of your science department. The questions and activities given above exemplify the way you might go about this. We encourage you to write your own questions and activities if you consider those suggested here unsuitable for your department.

2.2	Images of science

Purpose:

The purpose of this set of activities is to review the variety of ways in which science is presented to your pupils and the image of science that your department projects within the school.

Activity:

1   Produce a proforma which asks colleagues to list the styles of teaching they use. You might offer some examples, e.g.:

   ●   question/answer session
   ●   answering text book questions
   ●   dictation
   ●   poster work
   ●   analysis of secondary sources
   ●   role play/simulations around controversial issues

2   Find out what styles of teaching the pupils recognise and consider to be motivating.
   Design a matrix to match the coincidence of pupil perceptions and teaching styles identified by science colleagues.

3   What image of science do pupils get when they walk into the science department?
   Write a brief description.
   Ask pupil(s) from each year group to describe how they perceive the science department.
   Compare perceptions.
   Now consider what kind of image you wish to project to pupils.

4   What is the image of the science department in the school?
   Conduct a brief survey of other staff attitudes. This could be a broad sample of staff using semi-structured interviews, or it could be a short questionnaire to all (or most) staff with questions derived from two or three interviews.

5   Identify any science department activities which are seen to make a positive contribution to the school as a whole.
   Identify any negative contributions.
   What image of science does the science department wish to project within the school?
   What do you need to change to achieve this?

Notes:

You will need to act sensitively in some of the above areas. Science colleagues' perceptions of the image of the science department may well be at odds with pupil perceptions or the perceptions of other colleagues within the school.

Acknowledging science teachers' professional knowledge —————— 2.3

Purpose:

The purpose of this activity is to give recognition to the particular kind of professional knowledge that is firmly rooted in the science teacher's understanding of the subject matter.

Activity:

Science teachers often know more than they think; but do they value this kind of professional knowledge?

1   Read pages 36 - 38 which deal with teachers' professional knowledge, and with pedagogical content knowledge in particular.

2   The following questions are designed to get colleagues to think specifically about the kind of knowledge they possess which is rooted in their understanding of the subject matter. There are many more you might wish to pose which are perhaps better suited to your science department.

   ● How are your decisions about classroom management informed, guided or determined by your knowledge and understanding of the subject matter?

   ● What kinds of metaphors, models, analogies, anecdotes, narratives do you invoke to enliven your science teaching?

   ● How do you deploy such representations in the classroom?

   ● What use do you make of children's conceptions (and misconceptions) in science to structure or sequence activities?

   ● How do you use such knowledge to structure question and answer sessions or to create activities which require pupils to move beyond recall and develop their understanding of the subject matter?

   ● In what ways do you use your knowledge of the nature of science to develop pupils' thinking skills?

   ● How do you take advantage of critical incidents related to subject matter which occur in the laboratory? (See 'Critical Incidents in the Science Classroom', *M Nott & J J Wellington, School science Review, 1995, 76[276]*)

   ● How do you use your knowledge of IT to stimulate pupils' understanding of the limitations in the use of theoretical models?

3   Think about these questions and then try to think of examples from your teaching.

Notes:

Pedagogical content knowledge is a term which embraces a variety of forms of knowledge that effective science teachers draw upon to structure and inform their lessons. It is about how the subject matter is manipulated and transformed into activities which have the capacity to stimulate and motivate the pupils.

Set aside a regular time in departmental meetings, teacher development days etc. for colleagues to report on techniques where they believe they have made creative and imaginative use of the subject matter in order to motivate the pupils.

If access to a camcorder is possible, encourage colleagues to record clips for use as in-service material.

Section Three

Where are we now?

Sections One and Two have introduced the major factors we believe are highly influential in determining whether effective learning in science takes place. If these factors are taken on board the next step is to establish where your department is now. The purpose of this section is to offer strategies to enable you to determine where your department is in relation to these factors, and to help you guide it where you want it to go.

Helpful starting points include:

- **asking yourself what you believe about effective learning**
- **reviewing Schemes of Work (SoW)**
- **discovering pupils' perceptions of where you are now**

For each of these areas, we have suggested possible activities which could form part of a department meeting, an INSET day or be fitted in at other times.

Activity 1   What do you believe about effective learning?

What do your colleagues think makes for effective learning? And is it the same as, or related to, effective teaching? How do you know when learning has been effective?

The aim of this activity is to establish what range of views about effective learning exist in your department. Our contention is that unless there is some degree of consensus within a science department about what constitutes effective learning, the imposition of one view, for example, by the Head of Science, is unlikely either to prevail or to work. Agreeing principles is a prerequisite for the successful implementation of change.

Some statements about effective learning

	AGREE	UNDECIDED	DISAGREE
● Pupils who are pro-active or take responsibility for their learning will become effective learners			
● Those pupils who respond well to questions at the end of the lesson indicate that effective learning has taken place			
● Effective teaching will lead to effective learning			
● There are many approaches to learning; some are more effective than others			
● Effective learning only occurs when the teaching style coincides with the pupil's preferred learning style			
● Low ability pupils will never be effective learners			
● Pupils should be free to learn in the way they think is most effective for them			
● Effective learning takes place when teachers have a clear/coherent theory about how pupils learn			

This activity presents a set of twenty different statements about effective learning, some of which are shown on the previous page. These statements appear in the Appendix p.99-101, where they are presented in two forms – as a questionnaire and as a sheet to be cut up into cards.

Part A: **Individual exercise:** the purpose of this exercise is to give members the opportunity to respond individually to the statements on the questionnaire as agree, disagree or undecided. The organiser collects in the completed forms and analyses them for patterns, agreement, disagreement, and feeds back the outcome to the members for discussion. This could be before, during, or after the second part of the activity.

Part B: **Collaborative exercise:** the purpose here is to share ideas and to explain to others the reasoning underpinning them. Members work in pairs and group the statements on individual cards under whatever headings are deemed appropriate. The outcomes should be presented on a piece of poster paper. If possible, pairs should join in to fours and produce a consensus poster.

Following appropriate discussion it is then the responsibility of the organiser to use the analyses to frame a set of principles with which the majority feel comfortable. These principles should guide and underpin schemes of work and other curriculum or policy documents.

Activity 2   Reviewing schemes of work

In most schools in the UK there is a requirement that the content of the curriculum will be presented in the form of 'schemes of work' which are generated by the science department itself. Such schemes of work, each representing a particular course of study, must be intelligible to governors and parents (and OFSTED inspectors) as well as acting as the working documents for the science staff responsible for teaching the National Curriculum.

Typically a scheme of work ought to be a practical guide which:

- **translates curriculum aims into practice**
- **allows teachers to share and develop curriculum expertise**
- **provides a resource from which teachers can plan, teach and assess**
- **demonstrates continuity and progression in the content**

The format any particular scheme of work takes, however, is for each individual science department to determine; there are no hard and fast rules which must be applied. The approach employed for the generation of schemes of work will be contingent on a range of factors, e.g. staff expertise, enthusiasm and attitudes, special needs provision, technical help and resources, facilities, nature of pupils and so on. In this book we take the view that each science department is unique and has a unique set of factors that determine the approach taken and we would not wish to suggest a universal model.

We would, however, advocate that schemes of work reflect what each team of teachers responsible for teaching a course believes the nature of that course should be, and which incorporate the principles established through an activity, as has been suggested above. To achieve this end we suggest each team should arrive at a consensus about what a scheme of work should comprise, through a review process that considers the factors influencing effective learning highlighted in Section One. There is no reason why all schemes of work must follow a common format, but for ease of use a department may generate a format to which all teams conform.

The starting point might be to bring current schemes of work together and subject them to an analysis. Below is a list of questions which could be used as a framework. (See Appendix for a proforma list which could be used or adapted for this audit).

Reviewing schemes of work

Does the SoW currently:	Yes	No	Action to be taken
● provide an overview/links with NC?			
● show how the content has been analysed?			
● identify the major concepts and show how they are related to one another?			
● identify previous knowledge/concepts/skills required?			
● make learning objectives and success criteria explicit?			
● show learning pathways through tasks and activities?			
● show conceptual progression?			
● show where formative assessment should occur?			
● point out where children usually experience difficulty?			
● give typical pupil misconceptions?			
● show how assessment framework reflects relative emphases placed on skills, knowledge and understanding?			
● identify safety issues/relevant Hazcards?			

Following the review, departments can identify areas in which further development is necessary. This is likely to involve the structure, organisation and content of the scheme of work. Section Four contains useful ideas for the department seeking agreement on changes.

Activity 3   Pupils' perceptions of where you are

If the evidence presented in Section One is accepted as valid then clearly establishing what pupils think is an essential starting point for any review process. A review may focus on one or more aspects of what pupils think. Data could be collected through simple pencil-and-paper exercises in class or as homework. This could be collected anonymously which may give more open responses than if names are attached. Pupils must be clear that these exercises are not tests but are for a different purpose to help their learning.

More detailed information can be obtained through interviews but there are problems in finding the time for this and there is also an issue concerning the validity of the data if teachers interview their own pupils. It may be possible to support some teacher time through INSET funding or it might be possible to negotiate the involvement of student teachers in data collection, for whom it could be a valuable and mutually beneficial activity. There are some sensitive ethical issues if data is collected about attitudes relating to different teachers. These need to be worked through in advance and nothing should be done without the agreement of all those concerned.

Here are a few ideas of areas for investigation:

 A **Surveying pupils' levels of interest/motivation/enjoyment**
Carry out an attitudinal survey which would seek responses to how the pupils feel about science in general and the subject matter in particular.

Collecting children's views

"I liked this topic a lot.." | "I liked this topic.." | "I neither liked nor disliked it.." | "I didn't like this topic.." | "I didn't like this topic at all.."

Feeding back the analysis of responses to a small group of pupils to get them to comment on the results could give some further insights. This will also act as a validity check and get at clarification/articulation, insights into their responses.

 B **Surveying pupils' perceptions of teaching strategies**
As a consequence of the previous exercise questions concerning teaching styles and pupils' preferred ways of learning might be investigated.

Present a short list of teaching styles which are used in your department and ask the pupils to rank them in order of preference.

What do you prefer to do in lessons?

- Answer teachers' questions ☐
- Make posters ☐
- Copy from the board ☐
- Discuss questions in a small group ☐
- Make notes from a video ☐

Surveying pupils' learning styles

Use a questionnaire based on the different types of learning styles discussed in Section One. **'Educating for Capability'**, *Gordon Bell (RSA, 1991)*, contains a learning styles exercise based on David Kolb's work. An extension might be to survey teachers' learning styles at the same time!

D ▶ Investigation of pupils' perceptions of level of challenge

Practical work can often be unfocused if its purposes are not well thought through. Pupils then find it hard to explain why they are doing it.

Arrange for a colleague/novice teacher to circulate during one of your lessons and ask pupils to talk about why they are doing the practical work. Can pupils explain:

- **how the practical work illustrates or exemplifies theory?**
- **what kind of outcomes they are looking for and why?**
- **how the practical work helps them (or not) to understand/learn science?**
- **what they find hard or easy?**
- **its relevance to their lives/the world outside the science laboratory?**

E ▶ Survey of pupils' perceived need for the whole picture

Revealing the subject/topic piece by piece rather than being allowed to see the whole picture at the outset is a common criticism of how school science is presented to pupils.

Set up small group discussion. Get pupils to prepare a poster to explain how they would like a topic presented to them. If possible, record one of their discussions.

Do it for real? Start a topic by asking the class how they would like to start! Let children come up with questions they would like answered.

F ▶ Eliciting childrens' ideas

Some ideas for doing this were presented in Section One. More detailed guidance is contained in the Support Materials for Teachers which go with **'Making Sense of Secondary Science'**, *R Driver, et al (Routledge, 1994)*, although this is quite expensive. There are also some useful appendices in **'Learning in Science'**, *R Osborne & P Freyburg (Heinemann, 1985)* which deal with finding out about childrens' ideas in general and also give some specific examples of questions on several topics.

Educational research can be a minefield when it comes to being confident about your data and the conclusions you draw from it, but these exercises should give some useful indications of how pupils feel about their experience of science at present and how that compares with your own perceptions. They may thus help to suggest some possible areas which do need improvement. David Hopkin's book **'Classroom Research for Teachers'** *(Open University Press, 1995)* is a practical source of other ideas and provides a rationale for this sort of study.

Planning for effective learning

At the end of Section One, we articulated a set of principles for good practice. The intention in this section is to apply those principles in planning for effective learning. In particular we wish to:

- **present a paradox in the curriculum and challenge the orthodoxy in schemes of work that suggests 'everybody-does-everything'**
- **consider how a model of learning can be built into a scheme of work**
- **explore a range of strategies which could contribute to the planning of schemes of work**

This section considers how the principles of good practice set out in Section One should influence and guide the planning in the process of translating curriculum policy into the practical manifestations of classroom practice. For example, principles such as that of establishing a clear relationship between conceptual and procedural understanding require detailed planning that identifies how particular activities will deliver specific conceptual and procedural learning outcomes.

Furthermore, it is necessary to be clear about which learning model will be applied as this too will have implications which must be considered at the planning stage. It would be a nonsense, for example, to accept an experiential learning model but then fail to devise activities which can provide opportunities for pupils to learn experientially.

Before embarking on this planning stage, however, a much larger issue must first be tackled.

The curriculum paradox

The curriculum paradox can be first summed up by this view of the curriculum expressed by HMI in 1980.

> *The curriculum has to satisfy two contrary requirements. On the one hand it has to reflect the broad aims of education which hold good for all children, whatever their abilities and whatever schools they attend. On the other hand it has to allow for difference in the abilities and other characteristics of children, even of the same age.*

A View of the Curriculum *(HMSO, 1980)*

Whichever part of the UK we teach in, we have limited freedom to select content from wherever we please to build our curriculum for effective learning. All four countries have, to a greater or lesser extent, a prescribed 'national curriculum', although there is some variation in the overall structure and content. In England and Wales there has been a pendulum swing in both the structure and in the detail of specification of the content from the first version, which came out in 1989 with seventeen attainment targets areas and over 400 statements of

National Curriculum Science – the pendulum swings

attainment set in a complex ten-level matrix, to the 1995 version with four attainment targets and 36 level descriptions.

In England and Wales the content of the National Curriculum is defined by Programmes of Study which present the content to be taught in each phase or Key Stage. At the start of the document it states:

> *The programme of study for each key stage should be taught to the great majority of pupils in the key stage, in ways appropriate to their abilities.*

Science in the National Curriculum *(HMSO, 1995)*

The above statement seems to suggest that the programmes of study have to be taught in full to virtually all pupils. All that will be different will be the ways and means found by science teachers to achieve common goals and presumably the extent to which they are successful. If one studies the development of the National Curriculum and supporting documentation, it is clear that the intention and spirit of the original version was for all pupils to tackle basically the same areas of study but not to be aiming to reach the same attainment levels.

Challenging the orthodoxy

Our intention is to challenge the orthodoxy that suggests 'everyone-does-everything'. This notion seems to underpin many current linear curriculum plans by proposing some practical strategies which offer not only the potential for differentiation in terms of pupil access, but also in terms of conceptual and procedural understanding through the development of learning pathways.

In our view the key to meeting the needs of pupils of differing needs and abilities lies in a flexible interpretation of the Programmes of Study and a thorough analysis of the content in order to identify pathways through it which clearly show a progression of ideas and the relationships between key concepts. In this way pupils will cover the same area of study but at levels which vary according to their needs.

Such a curriculum plan must obviously be designed to satisfy the National Curriculum Programmes of Study, as they broadly define the content, and must emphasise a progressive coverage where key ideas are built upon and sound foundations are secured for subsequent study. The National Currciulum is not much help here as it merely states:

> *The numbers and letters throughout the programmes of study are for referencing purposes only and do not necessarily indicate a particular teaching sequence or hierarchy of knowledge, understanding and skills.*

Science in the National Curriculum *(HMSO, 1995)*

Clearly the responsibility is left with the science department in each school to sequence and organise the content with regard to continuity and progression, and to provide a sound basis for effective learning in science for the variety of pupils in its care.

Applying a learning model

An important initial stage of the planning is to ascertain what kind of 'learning model' will be adopted by your department. Sections One and Two introduced several aspects of current relevant and influential research about how children learn in general; this, together with current research in science education and learning theory as well as other factors, ought to be brought to the attention of the science department and taken into account. Each colleague is also likely to have his or her own implicit theories about how children learn science. But how can these be brought together to provide a coherent approach to sequencing and organising the content?

A learning model, informed by current research, should represent the view of how you and your department think children learn science, with individual theories brought out into the open so that all members from the department can share in the thinking process. Once made explicit the teaching strategies and approaches you adopt ought then to reflect the learning model.

Some different learning models were presented in Section One, in particular that developed by the Childrens' Learning in Science Project. The model shown below was developed in the RSA 'Educating for Capability' project, mentioned earlier.

The four stages of learning

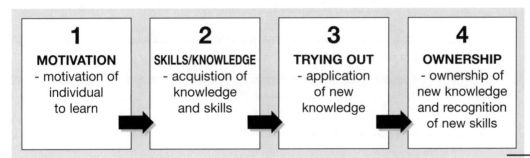

OHT14

Adapted from 'Educating for Capability: A Practical Guide', G Bell (RSA 1991)

If this, or any other, model is accepted then it should be reflected in some form in curriculum plans. At the very least a learning model or framework ought to be a set of shared guiding principles on which the organisation, the planning and the delivery of the science curriculum is based, and should be evident in the plans you write.

Planning a scheme of work

The aim of this section, therefore, is to offer a menu of practical approaches to planning which you might adopt, adapt or modify to meet the needs of your science department. The means and methods actually chosen to transform content into teaching material appropriate to different groups of pupils is for each science department to determine within its agreed framework.

The OFSTED inspection guidance has one particular view on planning which it is helpful to mention here. It states:

> *Good planning means that the teaching in a lesson or a sequence of lessons has clear objectives for what pupils are to learn and how these objectives will be achieved. It will take account of the differing needs of pupils. ... Whatever form planning takes, inspectors need to look for evidence of teaching intentions and how they will be met.*

Guidance on the Inspection of Secondary Schools *(HMSO, 1995)*

The Handbook is also quite specific in the kind of evidence it requires in order that inspectors may come to form judgements. Inspectors should look for evidence that planning:

> - *incorporates National Curriculum programmes of study, syllabus and course requirements;*
> - *sets out clear objectives;*
> - *summarises what pupils will do and the resources they will need;*
> - *shows how knowledge and understanding can be extended, and the work adapted to suit pupils who learn at different rates.*

Guidance on the Inspection of Secondary Schools *(HMSO, 1995)*

Since the introduction of the National Curriculum, the concept of a 'scheme of work' has become the accepted framework through which planning is executed. The non-statutory guidance that accompanied the 1989 version provides some very helpful guidance on creating schemes of work. It begins by emphasising collaboration and vision – a view we share and believe is fundamental if effective learning is to occur. It suggests:

> *In order to provide a coherent structure for the science curriculum in a school, it is essential that teachers have a shared vision of the purposes of their teaching. The development of the scheme of work, by teachers working together, is a mechanism whereby a coordinated approach can be achieved.*

Non-Statutory Guidance for Science *(NCC, 1989)*

The planning of a scheme of work clearly involves several stages if it is to incorporate a learning model and facilitate differentiation in a way that makes explicit the learning objectives and the learning routes through them. The Northamptonshire Inspection and Advisory Service in their book on differentiation in science reinforces the importance of schemes of work which should be considered here:

> *A scheme of work should be one of the single most effective ways of facilitating differentiation by the teachers in a department. As the central document that guides the teaching within a department the detailed scheme of work should contain a variety of information which promotes effective differentiation. Details of appropriate differentiation strategies included within the detailed scheme of work will reduce the amount of time individual teachers need to spend planning for differentiation in their lessons. Differentiation is essentially about having different learning objectives appropriate to the pupils in a class or different routes to achieving a common learning objective. Therefore learning objectives and learning routes should be documented with the scheme of work.*

The Differentiation Book *(NIAS, 1995)*

One thing we know about differentiation is that it is a planned process and it is important that planning starts with the scheme of work. Whatever approach we use, it will take time to develop. It would seem a more effective use of science teachers' time to be working on this, than writing worksheets at different levels. We suggest an approach here which we hope will open the way to the development of a collaborative spirit amongst colleagues.

In developing a strategy for producing a scheme of work, the temptation is to send the specialist teacher off to work on his or her own favourite area. However, if planning at this level is carried out by specialist teachers on their own the danger is that the tacit knowledge that is brought to bear on the organisation of the content, decisions about depth of treatment and sequencing will neither be made explicit nor shared with other colleagues in the final product. This strategy removes a valuable opportunity for department members to gain some professional development through curriculum development, particularly in the acquisition of *pedagogical content knowledge* (see Section Two).

The suggestion that more time needs to be invested in schemes of work will not go down well with many teachers who have spent considerable amounts of time on this already, only to find goalposts moved. However, the activity in Section Three on schemes of work may well have revealed areas which require further development, particulary if the department wants to have a clearer framework within which to make decisions about the activities pupils will do.

So what are the stages involved in planning a scheme of work?

We will deal with five areas:

1 **Creating an overview**
2 **Identifying a hierarchy of learning outcomes**
3 **Finding learning routes**
4 **Transformation**
5 **Identifying assessment opportunities relating to learning outcomes**

1 Creating an overview

Presenting a visual and accessible overall picture of a topic where the principal concepts and the relationships between them are identified is the starting point.

Our favoured approach here is concept mapping (see **'Learning how to learn'**, *J D Novak & D B Gowin (Cambridge University Press, 1984)*. Concept maps are two-dimensional diagrams which show how concepts are related to one another within a hierarchical form of organisation. Although the technique of concept mapping has been widely used as a diagnostic and assessment tool with pupils, it can also be used as an explicit way of analysing a topic to determine its constituent principal concepts and representing the relationships between those concepts in an open and readily accessible form. It should be seen as both a process and a product.

- As a process it is a highly effective way of bringing teachers together to collaborate, share knowledge and expertise and to develop their understanding of the content area under review.

- As a product it makes explicit the way an individual or a group perceive the inter-connectness of a group of concepts. The product is particularly important for colleagues, who were not part of the collaborative process, to gain an overview of how the concepts in a topic relate to one another and to probe the underlying rationale.

Curriculum planning through concept mapping

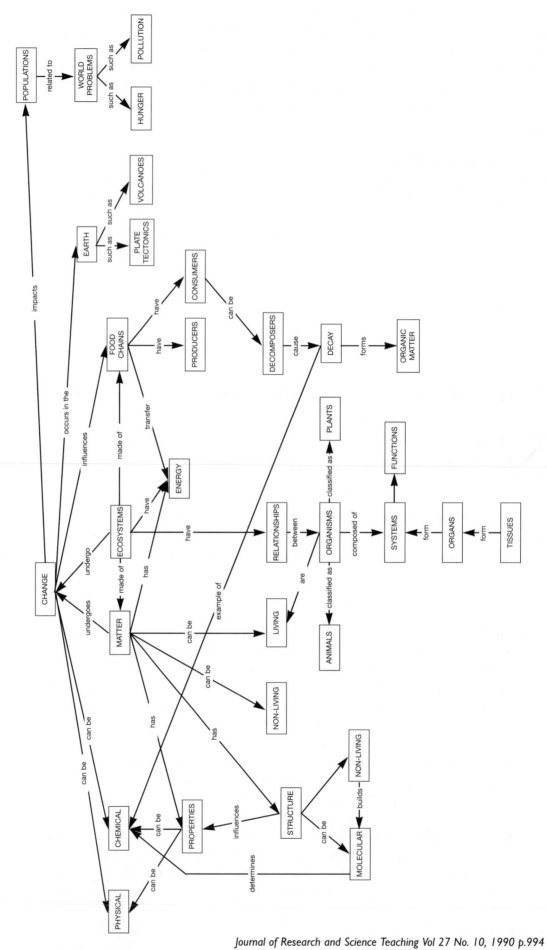

Journal of Research and Science Teaching Vol 27 No. 10, 1990 p.994

Effective Learning in Science

The concept map on the preceding page was developed by a group of sixth-grade teachers in the United States. This was their first version; through discussion and collaboration they eventually produced four versions – each one representing a further clarification of structure of the topic and relationships between the concepts.

Process and product together offer a powerful way of analysing a specific area of content. During collaboration each individual should try to make explicit the reasoning that underpins his or her view of the organisation of the concepts. In this way the discussion has the potential to lead to the establishment of a hierarchy of related concepts.

Once a map has been agreed it can be used to begin the identification of potential learning outcomes which in turn can form the basis of differentiated learning routes for pupil learning.

Maps can be created at a general level or at a highly specific level. For example, the topic of nutrition at Key Stage 3 (11-14 year age group) could be mapped at a general level with reference to ...

> ... food sources ...
> ... types of food ...
> ... diet ...
> ... uses of food in the body ...

... with links made to respiration, growth and excretion, whilst the process of digestion could be treated in more detail.

The technique of concept mapping is a useful and efficient means of creating an overview and identifying possible learning outcomes. Its provisional nature means that it can be readily updated or revised. Indeed advocates of the technique stress the value of the process of revision in terms of the generation of greater insight and understanding of the topic mapped. Collaborative concept mapping as suggested here could be a powerful tool for the transfer and acquisition of pedagogical content knowledge.

2 Identifying a hierarchy of learning outcomes

We have stressed the importance of clearly expressed learning outcomes in Section One. They will help to clarify the learning in science that you hope will take place. Moreover, if they are also presented to pupils there is a better chance they will share in the common goals and understand better what they are supposed to be doing. As far as possible, learning outcomes should indicate progression in both conceptual and procedural knowledge.

One approach is being used by Noadswood School in Hampshire which has developed a framework for assessment based on learning objectives set at three levels, shown over the page.

> ### The assessment framework
>
> Every assessment made of pupils' work is a measure of the extent to which a learning objective has been achieved by the pupil.
>
> ### Learning objectives
>
> Learning objectives are the fundamental elements within the scheme of work. They define the learning outcomes for pupils from the activities which the teacher plans. They are defined as **F** = foundation, **I** = intermediate and **H** = higher, and should be interpreted in the context of the level of study.
>
> ### Example
>
> ### Module - Living Things
>
> **F** - Distinguish between plants and animals, give examples of flowering/ non-flowering plants
> **I** - Construct simple branched keys to name everyday lab items.
> **H** - Distinguish between (an organism's) features which are inherited and those which have an environmental origin.

The aim in this stage is to write learning outcomes which represent some form of hierarchy. The American educator Robert Gagné recognised that many school subjects could be described hierarchically and that therefore it was important to ensure prior knowledge at 'lower' levels before attempting to teach something 'higher' – he used the idea of 'readiness' not just in the sense of being motivated but having the right conceptual foundations on which to build. The concept mapping process, if it has been carried out as suggested above, will yield a range of ideas which can form the basis of learning outcomes as well as suggesting some form of hierarchy. For this to work we need a framework that shows the progression of ideas. Teachers should be able to use their professional judgement to interpret the learning outcomes in terms of the level in which they are set.

> *Learning outcomes or learning objectives?*
>
> *We deliberately use the term learning outcome to avoid the mechanistic approach to curriculum organisation associated particularly with behavioural learning objectives. If we go too far down the road of using learning objectives we run the risk of only expressing what it is easy to describe in this way. This will generally direct us towards fairly low level factual knowledge or skills and away from higher cognitive levels and the affective domain. Learning outcomes may not be as tightly defined but they may encourage us to think about a more comprehensive and balanced view of what is to be learned.*

In their book **'Exploration: a way of learning science'** *(Blackwell, 1990)*, the authors A Qualter, J Strang, P Swatton and R Taylor consider progression of knowledge and understanding. They recognise four different ways used in the National Curriculum to define it which could be useful in developing hierarchies:

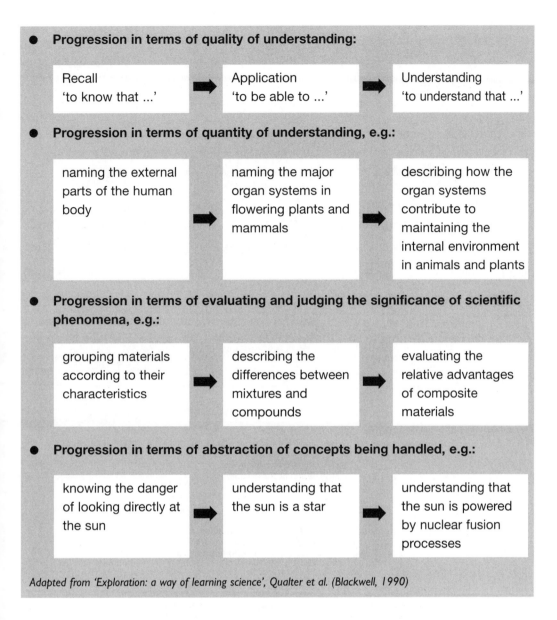

- ● **Progression in terms of quality of understanding:**

| Recall 'to know that ...' | → | Application 'to be able to ...' | → | Understanding 'to understand that ...' |

- ● **Progression in terms of quantity of understanding, e.g.:**

| naming the external parts of the human body | → | naming the major organ systems in flowering plants and mammals | → | describing how the organ systems contribute to maintaining the internal environment in animals and plants |

- ● **Progression in terms of evaluating and judging the significance of scientific phenomena, e.g.:**

| grouping materials according to their characteristics | → | describing the differences between mixtures and compounds | → | evaluating the relative advantages of composite materials |

- ● **Progression in terms of abstraction of concepts being handled, e.g.:**

| knowing the danger of looking directly at the sun | → | understanding that the sun is a star | → | understanding that the sun is powered by nuclear fusion processes |

Adapted from 'Exploration: a way of learning science', Qualter et al. (Blackwell, 1990)

A different approach is to draw on Bloom's well-known taxonomy of educational objectives to help establish a hierarchy of learning outcomes. The taxonomy is presented here to show how learning outcomes might be organised.

There are six levels in the cognitive domain of the taxonomy. Each level is accompanied here by a set of verbs which are offered to help distinguish between levels when writing outcomes. We have also included an example at each level:

1   **Knowledge – to name, state, draw, list**
    Example – pupils can draw a simple cell and label three major features

2   **Comprehension – to distinguish, classify, describe, give examples, summarise**
    Example – pupils can classify a group of materials into metals and non-metals and give reasons for the distinction

3   **Application – to relate, predict, modify, demonstrate how**
    Example – pupils can predict the presence of starch in a variety of supermarket foods and be able to explain why they expect them to contain starch

4   Analysis – to break down, compare, explain, infer, identify
Example – pupils can infer from a set of different velocity-time graphs which ones could represent a particular kind of activity (e.g. a dive) and why the others could not

5   Synthesis – to combine, construct, create, design
Example – pupils can design an investigation into enzyme mediated reactions which considers the interplay of two continuous variables

6   Evaluation – to appraise, compare and contrast, justify, interpret
Example – pupils can interpret the outcomes derived from an investigation into the relationship between mass and acceleration which do not match the outcomes predicted by the theory

In each case attainment will depend on the context in which the learning outcomes were set. For example, the distinctions required for the classification of the metals and non-metals will vary according to how the level is interpreted. The suggestion here is not to use this as a rigid or inflexible framework, but to offer a way of thinking about how learning outcomes might be phrased before being transformed into the content of teaching or tasks and activities.

Pyramid of learning outcomes

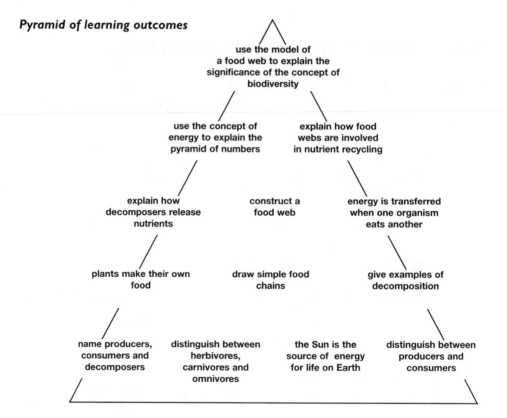

3 Finding learning routes
Having established a hierarchy of learning outcomes some form of diagrammatic representation is needed to see what the entry points and the routes might be according to the needs of different pupils.

This sort of representation of learning routes is the basis for Bloom's model for 'Mastery Learning'. This highly structured approach to planning for learning is discussed in the context of science in Keith Postlethwaite's book **'Differentiated Science Teaching'** *(Open University Press, 1993).*

Creating learning pathways

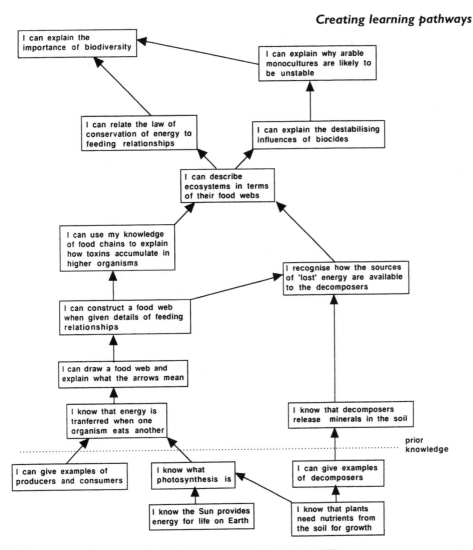

The Differentiation Book (Northamptonshire Inspection and Advisory Service, 1995)

The learning map may be quite general, or you might wish to break the area of study into smaller components and create two or more learning maps. The decision will depend on factors such as the nature of the subject matter and the perceived need to go into detail.

The routes will depend on the earlier analysis of the outcomes. The area of study will be the same for all the pupils but clearly the higher order objectives will be reached by fewer pupils and not all pupils may necessarily start at the same point. The aim is to provide pupils with different, but appropriate levels of challenge.

The link to assessment

At this stage the link to assessment becomes very important and should be identified on the learning map. Having a clear idea of the demands being made on the pupils through the need to attain specified learning outcomes will assist the identification of those points for diagnostic, formative and summative assessment. These points are taken up below.

4 Transformation

With the learning model guiding the thinking, the purpose of this stage is to find appropriate ways for the pupils to achieve the learning outcomes through the transformation of the content into the range of activities for teaching.

The use of the word activity is intended to be inclusive of all forms of representation undertaken by teachers or pupils. An activity, for instance, may be, inter alia, a highly structured question and answer session, a brainstorming session, a DART (Directed Activity Related to Text) exercise, an illustrative practical, the exploration of an analogy or model, or a piece of investigative work.

The choice of such activities designed to achieve learning outcomes will depend on the available resources and the management framework being operated. We will focus specifically on these latter elements in Sections Five and Six.

One approach to the process of transformation is shown below. This approach takes the learning map as the source of learning outcomes (LOs) to be achieved. From those LOs an activity chart is compiled where the activities are considered to have the potential to satisfy one or more LOs. Once identified the activities would undergo further analysis via strategies such as Vee mapping (see p.64-65) to assess their full potential.

Transforming the content

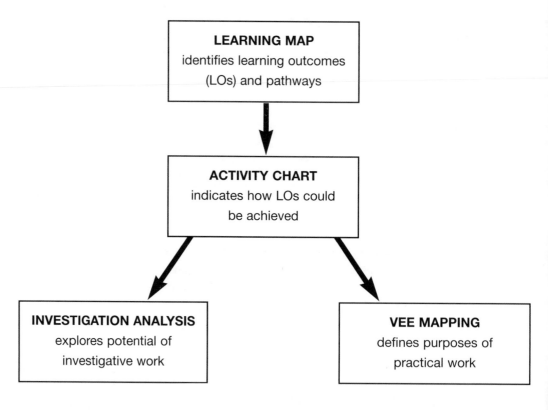

Critical in this process of selecting activities is the incorporation of the pedagogical content knowledge of the specialist teachers. It is their (otherwise tacit) working knowledge shared with their colleagues that should transform the subject matter into activities which have the potential to stimulate the curiosity of the pupils and motivate them to learn. As discussed in Section Two, it is knowledge of the history of the subject matter, its human aspects as well as its anecdotes and analogies, its metaphors and models which can revitalise a topic and to which the non-specialist needs access. Our view is that there is a synergy in this collaborative process where the product is greater than the sum of it parts. Not only can it stimulate the subject specialist by presenting his or her ideas to others, but the interaction between colleagues can lead to the development of ideas that would otherwise not have taken place. This may particularly be the case when a scheme of work is being produced for a topic which crosses the traditional subject boundaries. The classic example is 'energy' where the perspectives from biologists, chemists, physicists and geologists could all make a valuable contribution. But the same gains could be had by thinking about other big ideas such as particle theory which links to all areas of science.

Developing an activity chart

The first strategy we identify is the development of an activity chart. In any content area a range of activities determined by the learning model in operation (if there is one) will already form the current basis for classroom practice. In this stage it is important that we start with the LOs from the learning map and consider how they can be best achieved. Note that this is the other way around to most practice. We acknowledge, however, that this is a two way process, and knowledge of activities informs what is possible. This diagram shows how the process might be started:

Activity chart – identifying activities from learning pathways

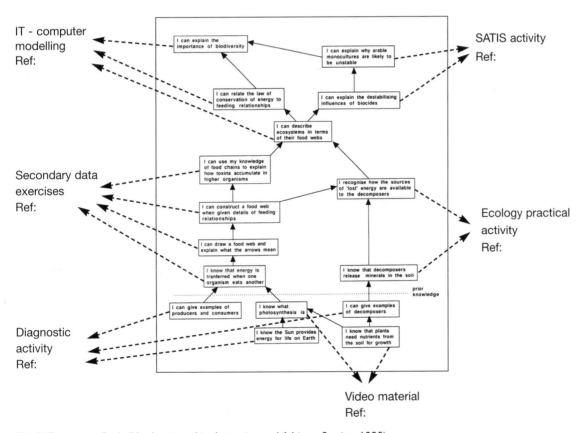

The Differentiation Book (Northamptonshire Inspection and Advisory Service, 1995)

The development of the activity chart should be a collaborative process to benefit from each teacher's PCK (pedagogical content knowledge). It might also be informed by what we have termed Bell's 4Cs and Claxton's 3Rs (see p.34). Finding opportunities to promote creativity and to develop pupils' abilities to transfer knowledge to novel and unexpected situations would be a great step forward in science education.

It will be very important in the construction of the activity chart to relate activities not only to the relevant learning outcomes but also to the model of learning which

---

underpins the framework. How this is done will depend on the model:

- If you are using the constructivist approach, then will activities in the early parts of the topic provide opportunities to bring out childrens' ideas?

- If you are using an experiential learning model, how do activities relate to its phases?

Decisions will also need to be made about teaching organisation. Which activities will be whole class? Which ones will be done in small groups? Is there any possibility of allowing any pupil choice?

Another approach has been used by the Longman/Nuffield 'Pathways through Science' scheme which is discussed in the ASE publication **'Managing Differentiated Learning and Assessment in the National Curriculum**, *(ASE, 1994)*. The key here is seen in breaking the scheme of work down into short units or 'episodes'. The advantages claimed are that:

- *Learning outcomes can be based on short-term goals, thereby improving motivation;*

- *a range of entry points is possible allowing schemes to be personalised to the individual pupil, and based on that pupil's prior experiences;*

- *pupils can be given a high degree of autonomy within the learning process by selecting their own route through materials;*

- *progress can be monitored across both short time frames and long time frames, ensuring that the most appropriate routes are always selected;*

- *regular target setting/profiling can easily be accommodated with this system, feeding in data to the Record of Achievement, but also encouraging continual, formative assessment.*

The next stages are designed to evaluate the potential of the activities as well as determining the range of LOs they may be able to deliver and establishing clearly for teachers and pupils what the purposes of the activity are. Practical work, in particular, has come under such severe scrutiny and criticism in recent times that it is important to articulate clearly why work of this kind should be undertaken. Investigation analysis and Vee mapping (see p.64-65) are two practical strategies which can help to ensure activities are purposeful.

Investigation analysis

Some of the activities shown will involve procedural as well as conceptual outcomes. The importance of bringing together these complementary demands in activities was stressed in Section One. This applies especially to 'investigations' of the type expected in the Programme of Study for Sc1. In **'Exploration: a way of learning science'** (See Bibliography) the authors suggest a very useful way of thinking about how investigations can be analysed in a way that shows progression from two perspectives – which they call 'task approach' and 'task complexity'. An element within the latter is the conceptual burden – the extent to which the activity requires understanding of scientific concepts – thus bringing together the procedural and conceptual dimensions.

Progression in investigations: the relationship between task approach and task complexity

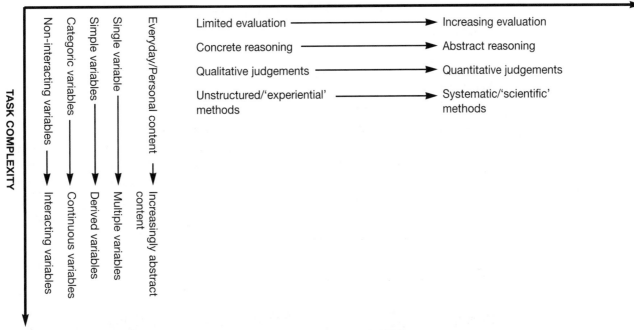

Adapted from 'Exploration: a way of learning science', Qualter et al. (Blackwell, 1990)

The diagram below shows how investigations in the same topic area can be set up in many ways (task approach) yet at the same time can vary in their procedural and conceptual demands (task complexity). This can provide a framework for progression and for differentiating these activities. This example illustrates the idea applied to investigations on electrical circuits:

Analysing investigation

TASK APPROACH

TASK COMPLEXITY

Problem A
Children are given a simple circuit (bulb, wires and a variety of batteries of different voltages) and asked to find out which is the best battery for lighting the bulb.

1 They test the first battery and find that it lights the bulb and state that it is the best battery.

2 They test all the batteries and note tht they light the bulb to differing extents and make a judgement once the whole series has been tested.

3 They test all batteries systematically, having devised a trial order in advance. Observations are repeated to check accuracy of judgements and batteries are ranked according to success in lighting the bulb.

Problem B
Children are given a circuit containing batteries, switches bulbs and wires, and asked to find out which of the components are faulty.

4 They randomly change components until eventually by chance, they discover the faulty component.

5 They try out one component at a time, until they find the faulty component.

6 They devise a plan in advance to ensure that all possible combinations of components are tested. They confirm their result by repeating as necessary.

Problem C
Children are given the components to complete a circuit, a voltmeter, ammeter and several pieces of wire of the same material but different diameters. They are aked to find out the relationship between wire diameters and electrical resistance.

7 They test the thinnest and thickest wires and state which one allows the greatest current through.

8 They test all the wires and measure the current flowing through each. They generalize the relationship.

9 They test all the wires, repeating measurements to allow for experimental error. Voltage and current used are measured and resistance computed. The data is represented graphically and a full generalisation provided.

'Exploration: a way of learning science', Qualter et al. (Blackwell, 1990)

Problem C requires substantially more theoretical background than Problem A in order for the investigation to be undertaken. The learning outcomes for Problem C can be expressed in both procedural and conceptual terms as the cognitive demand for both of them is high. Generalisation is a high order thinking skill which is not required for Problem A. Developing a matrix like this could be a useful extension of the activity chart to provide differentiated opportunities for investigations which integrate procedural and conceptual understanding.

Vee mapping

Another technique to analyse how an activity can be used to allow pupils to achieve agreed learning outcomes is Vee mapping (see **'Learning how to learn'**, *J D Novak & D B Gowin, Cambridge University Press, 1984)*. For our purposes, it is again a technique which has the additional benefit of bringing together the conceptual and procedural knowledge bases through the focus of clearly stated learning outcomes or questions. It is a very powerful but demanding technique which requires careful thought. As with concept mapping, this technique has been used by students to assess understanding as well as by teachers for curriculum analysis.

A Vee map for food and energy

CONCEPTUAL   FOCUS QUESTION(S)/   PROCEDURAL
LEARNING OUTCOME(S)

Theory/Principles:
- Energy is potential or kinetic
- Energy can be transferred, it cannot be created or destroyed
- Foods are potential sources of energy

FOCUS QUESTION(S)/ LEARNING OUTCOME(S)

Different foods vary in their richness as sources of energy

Knowledge claims:
- Different foods have different energy values
- Positive correlation between percentage fat and energy value
- Foods with higher percentage of fat have higher energy values

Concepts:
- Potential energy
- Fat, protein, carbohydrate
- Heat
- Food (source of potential energy)
- Energy value, joule, kilojoule
- Specific heat capacity
- Composition of food – percentage fat

Transformation:
- Calculation of energy transferred to water
- Calculation of energy transferred per g of food

EVENT

Burning peanuts, almonds, brazil nuts, cobnuts in bunsen flame underneath a fixed volume of water.

Data:
- Temperature mix – temp. before – temp. after (^{0}C)
- Mass of food (kg)
- Volume of water (ltr)
- Control variables stated and conditions specified

Placed in the centre as the starting point for the Vee map are the learning outcomes or focus questions to be addressed. This is deliberate and crucial as the tasks or activities must be seen as being subordinate to the learning outcome(s). Theory and practical need then to be considered in tandem so that the purposes of any activity (like practical work) and its associated knowledge base are seen to be serving the attainment of the outcome together. (See Professional development activity 4.3, p.70.)

This approach is an example of one that is underpinned by the belief that curriculum planning should be outcome driven and that appropriate forms of analysis should be employed to ensure that all activities, and practical activities in particular, have a clear sense of purpose for both teachers and pupils. Again this relates to our principles for effective learning in Section One.

5 Identifying assessment opportunities relating to learning outcomes

Building assessment into the planning stage is essential if it is to be truly an integral part of the learning process rather than a 'bolt-on'. The learning outcomes provide the starting point for the assessment framework which is designed to reflect their relative importance. Assessment instruments ought also to reflect the learning model that has been identified. For example, if a learning model is being applied which requires pupils' alternative ideas to be elicited, then appropriate diagnostic tests should be identified. If the learning model recognises that pupils have different preferred learning styles then the tests (formative and summative) should be selected and designed to embrace them; in other words there will not be the traditional uniformity. If emphasis is placed on the historical and human aspects of the development of science as a body of knowledge, then tests should provide opportunities for that to be assessed.

Where possible the assessment instruments ought to be written at the time the scheme of work is produced. Instruments may be required to assess different learning routes. An overview of the scheme of work will indicate where assessment is intended and what purpose it is to serve. All instruments can then be evaluated by other colleagues for fitness of purpose and degree of articulation with stated learning outcomes.

In this assessment stage of the planning process we focus on three major forms of assessment:

- **diagnostic**
- **formative**
- **summative**

Diagnostic assessment

Diagnostic assessment is a specific case of formative assessment in that it provides vital information to the science teacher who can then promote effective learning through informed teaching. It is a central component of 'Mastery learning' (see p.59).

The 'Children's Learning in Science' project and many other studies outline in considerable detail the difficulties pupils encounter in science. For example the CLIS project covers major topics such as energy, particle theory and plant nutrition, renowned for their conceptual difficulty. The materials referred to in Section Three offer a wealth of diagnostic tests which can be applied directly or used as a source of ideas for adaptation or modification.

Diagnosing misconceptions about dissolving

Sugar and Water

200g of sugar are put in to 1000g of water in a bowl. The water is stirred until the sugar cannot be seen.

a) The contents of the bowl will now have a mass of: (Tick one box.)

☐ A less than 1000g

☐ B 1000g

☐ C more than 1000g but less than 1200g

☐ D 1200g

☐ E more than 1200g

b) I chose this answer because:

....

....

CLIS, University of Leeds

In the example on the left children are given the opportunity to express their ideas by responding to a question relating to a simple activity about dissolving. It could be enacted in a lesson or it could be administered as a pen and paper exercise. Either way the information elicited could be used to inform the teaching process.

Formative assessment

The purpose of formative assessment is to provide feedback to the pupils in ways which show how they can improve. This is the crucial point. If pupils are unable to see how to achieve a learning outcome then they need access to 'staging posts' which will sign the way to success. Formative assessment can appear under a variety of guises, the choice of which depends on the learning model being used and the nature of the area of study. Whatever is chosen, the purpose needs to be clearly stated.

Formative assessment, for example, might be a homework task that requires pupils to explain differences in predicted and actual outcomes from an investigation, such as that shown below (this could be first-hand or second-hand data). Their performance in the task will alert you to their relative capabilities in handling the thinking skills. The feedback given to them will be the key to further progress.

Getting children to think

Julie is asked to pour precisely 20 cm³ of water into each of these containers.

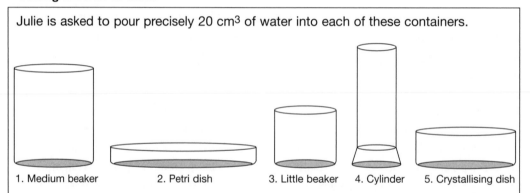

1. Medium beaker   2. Petri dish   3. Little beaker   4. Cylinder   5. Crystallising dish

She is then asked to measure the surface area and depth of water in each container. The table below shows the surface area of water but not depth.

Predict the order of depths of water Julie would find in the different containers. Using the numbers 1-5 write your prediction in the table, with number 1 for the deepest.

Container	Surface area of water	Prediction of depth
1	30cm²	
2	60cm²	
3	20cm²	
4	3cm²	
5	40cm²	

If Julie was given another straight-sided container and asked to say which position it would be in the order, how could she do it without measuring anything?

CASE

Summative assessment

Summative assessment is designed to allow progress to be measured in some form. The tendency with national testing is for instruments to be written which measure what it is

Effective Learning in Science

easiest to measure. For example, measuring recall of facts is a simple procedure which will give an indication of what pupils remember. Ability to recall facts may not necessarily be a reliable indicator of levels of understanding.

A pupil, for instance, may be able to recall a definition of force which suggests that this is something which causes a body to change velocity or direction. However, if the same pupil is asked firstly, to mark on a diagram the direction of force on a ball at several points along its trajectory and then secondly, required to apply the concept to an unfamiliar situation, an entirely different picture may emerge.

The form of a summative instrument should be related closely to the learning outcomes which have been set for the pupils to attain. Like the other forms of assessment, if a learning model is being applied, that model should be reflected in giving pupils the opportunity to attain the stated outcomes in a variety of ways.

The following review offers a range of questions designed to examine whether the assessment framework being applied is in accord with the rationale or philosophy underpinning it.

- Do the learning outcomes and the learning map form the starting points for the assessment framework?

- Do the formative instruments and summative test items reflect the nature of the learning model?

- In what ways are pupils actively involved in the assessment process?

- Are diagnostic tests built into the assessment framework at points where conceptual difficulties are known to arise?

- To what extent are the outcomes from the formative instruments used to inform the construction of the summative test items?

- Is the range of learning styles fairly represented in the formative and summative tests?

- Is the relationship established between the procedural and conceptual knowledge represented in test items?

- To what extent do the summative tests discriminate in favour of the higher order cognitive skills?

- Do the summative test items reflect the range of skills developed through the scheme of work?

REVIEW OF SECTION FOUR

- What view is shared by your department about the nature of differentiation? Is the consensus focused on the idea that 'all pupils should do (learn) everything'? Is the development of a more sophisticated approach necessary?

- Having reviewed your schemes of work, what are the adequacies and inadequacies of the procedures you currently employ?

- With a vision for science education in the future, what should be the form and nature of schemes of work that will reflect that vision?

- If you are dissatisfied with the current approach to planning schemes of work, what approach will you take to promote the use of more flexible and dynamic planning techniques in the construction of new schemes of work?

- Is the current policy towards assessment one that allows feedback from pupils' learning to drive curriculum development?

4.1 ————————————————————————— Concept mapping

Purpose:
The purpose of this activity is to consolidate your understanding of the principles of concept mapping and to offer a simple exercise to get you started.

Activity:
It might seem more logical to start with a section of the programme of study, but it is probably better to get into the process of concept mapping through a simple exercise. Read pages 53-55 in Section Four which discuss how to create an overview using concept mapping

1   Choose a passage of text from a reference book which has plenty of concepts to manipulate.

2   List the concepts you think are important, plus any others which you think will help in the construction of the concept map.

3   Write down all the concepts on small, separate rectangles of paper.

4   Spread the pieces of paper on a flat surface. Group related concepts together, but try to rank them within groups so that the most inclusive concepts come first and the most specific, e.g. examples, come last.

5   Shuffle the pieces around to build a concept hierarchy in a 2-D array, in a way that represents your understanding of the subject matter. (See example on page 54.) Remember, there is no one right way of doing this.

6   Copy the array onto a large piece of paper (A3). Draw connecting lines.

7   Write words or phrases which validly connect the concepts to one another. If you are not sure what the connection is then either find out or don't make it.

8   Now try to make cross-links with validating phrases between concepts in different parts of the map.

9   If you are not a specialist in the topic ask a colleague to look at the concept map. Check for omissions, misconceptions and missed or invalid connections.

10   Update the map. Concept mapping is essentially a dynamic technique where the process is more important than the product.

Notes:
Concept mapping is a metacognitive activity built on constructivism. This means that it forces you to think about your own thinking and challenges your own conceptions of science. It is also designed to improve your relational knowledge, i.e. how concepts in science are related to one another and how they are interdependent. This is crucial knowledge for structuring teaching sequences.

A useful reference on concept mapping is **'Concept mapping: a multi-level and multi-purpose tool'**, *P Adamczyk, M Willson & D Williams, 'School Science Review' 76 (275) pp116-124.*

Differentiating practical activities ———————————————— 4.2

Purpose:

The purpose of this activity is to encourage you to explore the potential of standard practical activities to offer pupils different learning pathways.

Activity:

This is a powerful analytic technique that looks at progression through task complexity and task approach. Starting points and end points can be different using roughly the same equipment.

1   Look at pages 62-64 to get an idea how this activity can be approached.

2   Use an investigation drawn from one of your schemes of work. Or you might, for example, try out this activity with a simple investigation such as the standard one involving marble chips and acid.

3   Review the learning outcomes that would normally associate with the investigation you have selected.

4   Identify lines of progression and use them to:
     a) vary the demands, and thus, the complexity of the task;
     b) vary the approach by inventing several starting points.

Notes:

The activity is based on the investigation analysis derived from **'Exploration: A Way of Learning Science'**, *A Qualter, J Strang, P Swatton, R Taylor (Blackwell, 1990)*, pages 43-45.

4.3 ——————————————————————————— Vee mapping

Purpose:

The purpose of this activity is two-fold: to appreciate how the technique of Vee mapping can bring together conceptual and procedural knowledge bases; and to develop skills in Vee mapping.

Activity:

This is a demanding technique which requires some time. Choose a familiar practical activity to practise on.

1 Look at the example of a Vee map presented on page 64.

2 Choose a practical activity which you wish to map.

3 Draw a Vee on an A4 piece of paper turned landscape. Determine the intended learning outcomes or focus question and write them in the centre of the Vee.

4 Think through the conceptual knowledge base on which the practical activity is founded and enter it on the left of the Vee. This involves theory and concepts and must include the prior knowledge which pupils need to have in place. (See example p.64.)

5 In relation to the learning outcomes, decide what observations or other data you wish pupils to collect.

6 Decide how these data will be transformed or manipulated. Check that the conceptual understanding is present so that pupils will understand what they are doing. Enter this information at the bottom of the right side of the Vee.

7 On the right of the Vee, analyse the procedural (cognitive as well as psychomotor) knowledge base that will be generated. Start with the records, i.e. the data that the pupils will generate. Then work your way up the right hand side by deciding what transformations are necessary and whether the pupils have the appropriate knowledge to do them. Next, decide what knowledge, conceptual and procedural, will be generated as a result of the activity.

Notes:

Although at first sight it would appear that the Vee map separates the conceptual and the procedural knowledge bases, in fact its design requires that the two are considered in combination to generate a rationale for how the learning outcome or focus question is to be achieved by the pupils.

For more on Vee mapping, see **'Learning how to learn'**, *J D Novak & D B Gowin (Cambridge University Press, 1984).*

Effective use of resources

In the previous section we considered ways in which schemes of work could be developed to provide a framework for effective learning. We took this process through to selecting appropriate activities to achieve the learning outcomes we generated. The next stage in the process is to decide on what resources could best be used to support the activities. The purpose of this chapter is to:

- **review what is meant by the term 'resource'**

- **explore the relationship between resources and activities**

- **offer guidance on resource selection and production**

What is a 'resource'?

The word 'resource' can be applied to a large number of things. Some would argue that the teacher is the most important resource available to support learning in the

classroom. An emerging theme in this chapter is to think of ways to release the teacher to make best use of his or her specialist skills and knowledge. We could also think of apparatus and equipment as resources which pupils often use under guidance from other resources. However, the word is most usually used as a generic term to cover text and visual materials such as worksheets, textbooks, videos or more recently computer software and CD-ROMs. In this sense (which is the way we are thinking in this chapter) the term 'resource' is used when we are thinking principally of materials containing information of one sort or another. If we think of information collected from 'hands-on' experimental work as generating primary data, then resources often contain secondary data which might be in the form of printed text, pictures, diagrams, sounds or moving images with which we want pupils to engage to expand their knowledge and understanding.

Over the last twenty years there has been a broadening of the range of resources available for teaching science and of the range of media which contain them. Traditionally the emphasis has been on printed resources from commercially-produced books to school-produced worksheets.

At one time the textbook was probably the main resource used by teachers. Its function was to provide factual information and perhaps questions and exercises for pupils to work through. The Nuffield Science projects in the 1960s and 70s produced a different sort of textbook which integrated together 'theory' with instructions for practical activities. Other science textbooks were influenced by this approach and began to include practical work. In the last fifteen years or so, the presentation of information in textbooks has improved significantly in a number of ways: through the use of a larger number of illustrations and photographs; through more emphasis on layout and design; through the use of colour; and through greater attention being paid to issues of readability.

Using worksheets

Despite improvements in textbooks, science teachers in the UK always seem to have had a healthy scepticism for them and an uneasy relationship has developed which prevents them from placing too heavy reliance on this sort of material. For many, the introduction of the worksheet was seen as an essential addition to the range of resources available. Practically every science teacher must have produced a large number from their initial training onwards. Motivation was not only some dissatisfaction with textbooks and commercially available material but a desire to cope with the introduction of mixed-ability teaching. The advent of high-volume photocopiers, word-processing and desktop publishing has further supported the production of school-based materials.

A 'motorway model' of differentiated worksheets

A graded worksheet

Often the attraction of producing worksheets was that it was possible to write them at different levels for different abilities between sets or within classes. A common approach here is to write something suitable for the 'average' child and then produce a simpler version for the 'less able' and a more complex version for the 'more able'.

An alternative is the 'graded worksheet' where there is a progression of difficulty within the tasks or questions from the first ones which all pupils should be able to do through to more demanding ones at the end.

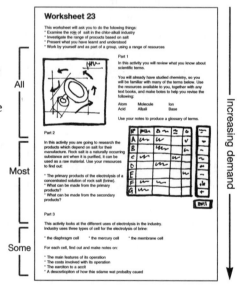

There are positive things about worksheets:

- They allow a more selective approach to the use of resources.
- They can be customised to the needs of the school (for example, regarding equipment).
- Consumable worksheets provide a paper record of work done by pupils.
- They may be a cheaper alternative to textbooks.

OHT15

But there are also several problems:

- They take to a lot of time to produce yourself.
- There is considerable variation in final quality.
- There is a limit to the use of colour, which makes them generally unattractive compared to textbooks.
- They often involve copyright infringements regarding illustrations and photographs!

With the advent of the National Curriculum all the major educational publishers have produced their own 'schemes' which often consist of a pupil textbook plus a teachers' guide with copyright-free worksheets. These are often designed to supplement core activities by providing simpler versions of activities as an alternative to those offered in the core book, or extension activities which are additional to those in the book.

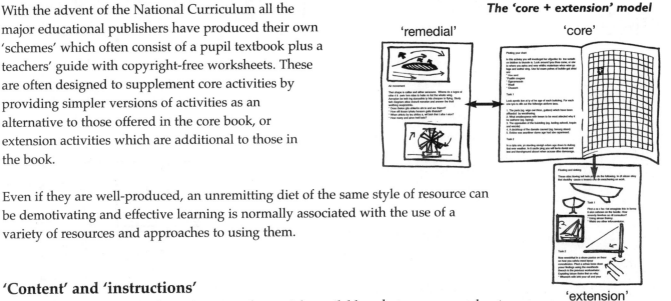

The 'core + extension' model

'remedial'   'core'

'extension'

Even if they are well-produced, an unremitting diet of the same style of resource can be demotivating and effective learning is normally associated with the use of a variety of resources and approaches to using them.

'Content' and 'instructions'

Against this background of a wide range of materials available, what can we say about resources for effective learning? The key features about effective learning discussed in Section One stressed the importance of recognising individual differences between pupils and responding to these when planning for learning. If pupils are working from resources then how can we pay attention to individual needs if they are working on the same worksheet or from the same page in the textbook, other than simply by noting the rate at which they work? If we are thinking about something like using CD-ROM or the Internet then it is unlikely that the whole class would be able to use the resource at the same time in any case. Perhaps what is needed is a more flexible approach to the use of resources. To give some ideas of how to do this let's start with worksheets and consider what's wrong with them!

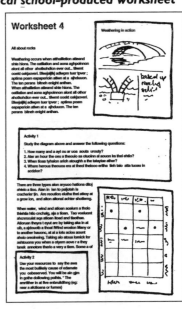

A typical school-produced worksheet

Take a typical worksheet – this might be a school-produced or commercial one. Look at the example on the right.

We can see two sorts of information in this worksheet. First, there is basic content information. This is in the form of text, a photograph and some diagrams. Second, there is instructional information which guides the pupil in what to do with the content information. It might be telling the pupil what to read or what to look at, to copy a diagram or answer some questions. Of course not all worksheets have this balance of the two sorts of information. The reality is that there is a continuum from 0% to 100% for each as shown in the diagram over the page.

At the left-hand side of the diagram would be examples which are 'pure content' in that they contain no instructional information at all. This would therefore need to be given

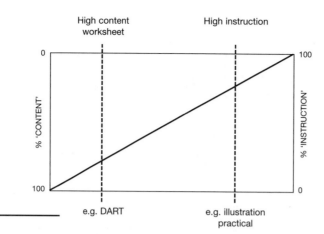

OHT16

by the teacher orally when the sheet is distributed or written on the board. At the right-hand end would be those worksheets consisting entirely of instructions, for example for practical work. In practice most worksheets are 'hybrids' – somewhere between these extremes, containing a balance of both sorts of information.

So is there a problem here? Let's consider the two types of information. The content information is probably taken from other sources in the first place and may need reworking and modification. Diagrams and photographs that have been through the photocopier lose definition and acquire thin black lines around the edges when we paste them up (apart from any copyright considerations!). Even with scanning devices and desktop publishing, the quality cannot hope to match the skills of a professional graphic designer. Children today, reared on a diet of television and computer graphics, would have to be highly motivated to respond enthusiastically to this sort of material.

Then there is the instructional information. Often the problem with a worksheet is not with the content information itself, it is with what we want the pupils to do with it. The instructions we give may not be clear, the questions we ask may not be pitched at the right level, and they may not make best use of the content presented.

Identifying 'content' and 'instruction'

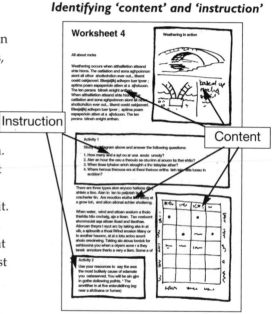

Flexible use of resources

If something is wrong with the content information or the instructional information on a stereotypical worksheet where the two are combined on the same piece of paper, then the only thing to do is to start again! But what would be gained by physically separating the content and the instructions into separate resources? How could this provide a more flexible approach? The idea of doing this is not new – a similar approach was first developed some time ago at the Resources for Learning Development Unit in Bristol. The RLDU employed a team of graphic designers to turn worksheets and other materials written by local teachers into a variety of small format booklets.

Small format print resources

Effective Learning in Science

In terms of the definitions above, many of these resources contained almost entirely 'content'. The instructional information was contained in 'task cards' which were separate A5 cards written to provide activities relating to the content resources.

The two together formed the key components of a 'management pack' consisting of a bank of content resources, a box of numbered task cards and a plan (shown below) to show how the two interrelated.

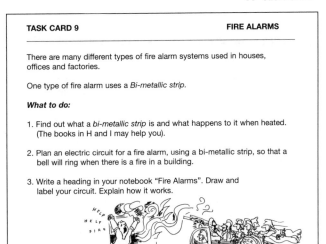

A 'task card'

TASK CARD 9   FIRE ALARMS

There are many different types of fire alarm systems used in houses, offices and factories.

One type of fire alarm uses a *Bi-metallic strip*.

What to do:

1. Find out what a *bi-metallic strip* is and what happens to it when heated. (The books in H and I may help you).

2. Plan an electric circuit for a fire alarm, using a bi-metallic strip, so that a bell will ring when there is a fire in a building.

3. Write a heading in your notebook "Fire Alarms". Draw and label your circuit. Explain how it works.

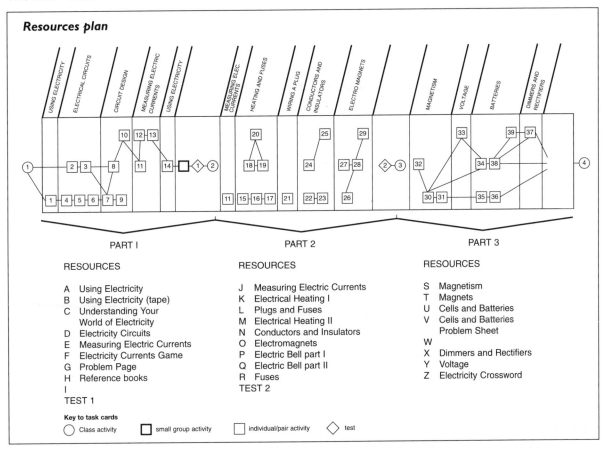

Resources plan

RESOURCES (PART I)

A Using Electricity
B Using Electricity (tape)
C Understanding Your World of Electricity
D Electricity Circuits
E Measuring Electric Currents
F Electricity Currents Game
G Problem Page
H Reference books
I
TEST 1

RESOURCES (PART 2)

J Measuring Electric Currents
K Electrical Heating I
L Plugs and Fuses
M Electrical Heating II
N Conductors and Insulators
O Electromagnets
P Electric Bell part I
Q Electric Bell part II
R Fuses
TEST 2

RESOURCES (PART 3)

S Magnetism
T Magnets
U Cells and Batteries
V Cells and Batteries Problem Sheet
W
X Dimmers and Rectifiers
Y Voltage
Z Electricity Crossword

Key to task cards

○ Class activity   □ small group activity   ▢ individual/pair activity   ◇ test

This approach which separates content resources from the tasks or activities that pupils carry out while using them has advantages over a worksheet scheme. The content resources were of higher quality than a school could produce and pupils responded well to them – in many cases better than to textbooks. The task cards did not just contain a series of questions which were basically about comprehension, as worksheets often do, but more challenging activities which required pupils to show their understanding of the content.

A number of similar task cards could be written at different levels with increasingly demanding activities, thus allowing 'differentiation by task'.

A task card could make use of one content resource or refer to a number of different ones, again perhaps graded by difficulty thus allowing 'differentiation by resource'.

Task cards 2 and 3 illustrate how the same resource item can serve the needs of pupils with differing abilities or interests.

TASK CARD 2   INTRODUCING MAGNETS

You will need: item T

What to do:

1. Write a heading in your notebook 'Magnets'

2. Read pages 1 to 10 of item T

3. Copy these questions into your notebook and answer them in complete sentences:

       a) How would you find out if a piece of metal was a magnet?
       b) What are the POLES of a magnet?
       c) What is a PERMANENT magnet?
       d) If a magnet is 'freely suspended' in what direction will the north pole of the magnet point. (page 6 will help you)
       e) Draw and label an early type of sailor's compass

TASK CARD 3   INTRODUCING MAGNETS

You will need: item T

What to do:

1. Write a heading in your notebook 'Magnets'

2. Read pages 1 to 12 of item T

3. Copy these questions into your notebook and answer them in complete sentences:

       a) The first magnets were pieces of black iron ore found near Magnesia, in Greece, as early as 600B.C. What would the Greeks notice that was special about the ore?
       b) What is a PERMANENT MAGNET?
       c) Many years ago sailors believed that their compass needles pointed to a magnetic island in the Arctic. Why do you think a compass needle always points in the same direction?
       d) Design and carry out a simple experiment to test out the idea that there is a close connection between electricity and magnetism. (Pages 11 & 12 of item T will help you. Also, look up the work of Oested in the science library)

The key note in this approach is flexibility; allowing a response to pupils' needs both through the challenge of the tasks themselves and by referring them to a variety of resources.

New resources can easily be integrated into a system like this. Single copy textbooks and reference books become useful classroom resources, as does the wealth of material produced by industrial and commercial organisations.

Task cards, if stored electronically, can be re-written, personalised or added to; with a worksheet often the only approach is to re-do the whole thing. The skills and time of the teacher can be channelled into developing tasks and activities matched to pupils' needs rather than into the inexpert production of content resources.

Obviously, there are a number of issues which arise using such a system: How do you monitor pupils' work to ensure they are all on task? What about safety? How do you keep track of resources and other equipment? These are basically classroom management problems which will be addressed in the next section.

Task cards requiring different resources

TASK CARD 34   CELLS & BATTERIES

You will need: item U

What to do:

1. Write a heading in your notebook 'Cells & Batteries'

2. Read pages 1 to 5 of item U

3. Copy the following questions into your notebook and write your answers.
     a) What is the difference between "a cell",and "a battery" (page 14 in item U will give you some extra information)
     b) What is needed to make a cell?
     c) Describe the first battery - the voltaic pile. (a labelled drawing will probably be the easiest way to do this).

4. Read pages 6 and 7 of item U.
Write a heading in your notebook "Making Cells"
Copy the diagram at the bottom of page 6.
Copy the 'results table' shown of page 7.

5. Make about 6 different cells, always using copper as one of the metals. Fill in the results table for each cell.

TASK CARD 35   INTRODUCING CELLS & BATTERIES

You will need: item V

What to do:

1. Write a heading in your notebook 'Cells & Batteries'

2. Read pages 1 to 4 of item V

3. Copy the following questions into your notebook and write your answers.

     a) What is the difference between a "cell" and a "battery" (see page 3)
     b) What is needed to make a cell?

4. Copy the cell drawn on the right, into your notebook and explain why it wouldn't produce an electric current.

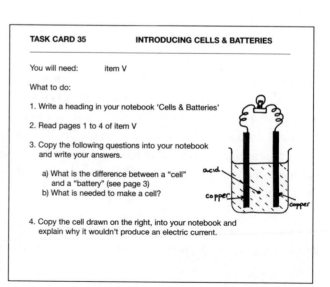

Effective Learning in Science

Study guides

An extension of the 'task card' approach is seen in the development of 'study guides'. In some ways a study guide can be thought of as an extended task card – it contains instructions for pupils to follow as they work through a series of tasks using separate resources. A series of materials produced by Network Educational Press exploit the potential of study guides.

The intention is that pupils working on their own or in small groups would use the guide to work through a number of activities covering a topic over a number of lessons. Key features of these guides include:

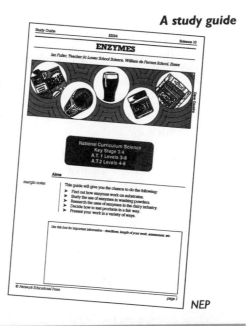

A study guide

NEP

● The use of advance organisers to present aims and learning outcomes clearly.

● A list of suggested resources is provided which could be added to or customised before the guide is photocopied for use.

● The guide has 'white space' to allow pupils and teachers to add additional information to define, clarify or extend tasks.

● The tasks themselves are presented in challenging ways which require pupils to research the topic for themselves rather than just answering a series of questions.

● The guides contain a number of prompts to help pupils get started and work through the activities.

● The activities are designed to generate some sort of 'product' but this is not always the normal sort of written account. It could be an oral presentation, a report designed for a particular audience, or even a video.

OHT17

The educational importance of these features is fully explored in Chris Dickinson's book **'Effective Learning Activities'** in this series.

If this approach is attractive it should be possible to produce similar study guides for other topics. The technical and production quality of this sort of instructional resource does not need to be high if it directs pupils to high quality content resources – these can include a wide variety from paper materials through to electronic media.

In science, the GCE A-level independent learning schemes – APPIL (Physics), ABAL (Biology) and ILPAC (Chemistry) are based on an extensive study guide through a whole topic, making use of a number of standard textbooks and other resources. These guides give some valuable ideas about the development of such instructional materials.

These and other similar developments have at their centre ideas about the learner working independently of the teacher's direct control and thereby taking some

---

responsibility and control over their own learning. Goals and learning outcomes are still determined by the teacher but routes to those goals can be determined to some extent by the learners themselves. Labels such as 'open learning', 'flexible learning' and 'supported self-study' are often attached to these developments and many schools and colleges are looking enthusiastically at them, particularly for older students in Further, Higher and Adult Education. Perhaps we could set some of the foundations for this in secondary education through the use of, for example, task cards in a structured way which will encourage the development of study and information skills and involve pupils more actively in their own learning.

Selecting resources

The picture that comes through the teaching approaches we have just discussed is that there may be a much wider range of resources required, and one which also, perhaps, involves a wider range of media.

In selecting resources, we need to have some criteria on which to base our judgements of suitability. Assuming that we are concerned with 'content resources' (as defined above), here are a few questions to think about:

1 *Does the resource match the learning outcomes for which I want to use it?*

This is fairly obvious but, if we have spent time in developing schemes of work as suggested in Section Four, then we will have clearly defined learning outcomes and we need to be sure that the resource contains relevant information related to them. Is it more suited to the needs of a particular group of pupils? Could different groups use different parts of it? Is it the best means to achieve the desired ends?

2 *Is the information the resource contains (text, pictures, data) going to be accessible to pupils?*

This is often seen in terms of 'readability' as applied to text. Whether text is readable or not is to do with a number of factors. Although the difficulty of language is a key one, a simple reading age formula does not give the full picture. Layout, design and typography can have an important influence as can the motivation of the pupils and the purpose for them reading it.

The concept of 'accessibility' is a broader one than 'readability' and could be applied not only to text but to other information forms. Accessibility is to do with the ease with which pupils can extract the information we want them to get. For example, how likely are the target group of pupils to absorb the information from a photograph or from a section of video or from data on a computer spreadsheet?

Related to this is the question of whether the resource is structured in a way that will allow the development of activities to go with it, particularly if the pupils are working semi-independently. This may apply to the new technologies – computer software, CD-ROMs etc. Could pupils easily be directed to key sections? Are special skills required to handle the media?

3 *What sort of 'images' are presented?*

This question can be interpreted in a number of ways. From the pupils' viewpoint, images in visual materials can 'date' very quickly. This is particularly true of videos. What was 'cool' last year is out today! Pupils' reaction to material is important, not only for reasons to do with fashion and style but in relation to the sorts of issues raised in Sections One and Two about gender and racial stereotyping. Textbooks and educational resources are much better than they were in terms of not always showing male scientists, and the representation of different ethnic groups in illustrations, but it is still worth thinking about the images of science and of scientists conveyed through the material and whether or not a better balance needs to be achieved.

Applying these sorts of criteria does not usually result in a straight YES/NO decision. No resource ever seems just right but addressing these questions may suggest ways in which it might be adapted.

Producing resources

So what of resource production? Despite the unhealthy desire many teachers have to rush into this, good advice is still probably...

... don't!

Why try to compete with professional graphic designers and educational publishers who have the time, training and technology to produce visually attractive materials?

Step 1   **Try to find a suitable professionally-produced resource.**

Step 2   **Try to adapt existing materials.**

Step 3   **Think about changing your classroom management to be able to use other resources.**

Step 4   **If all else fails – write something yourself!**

There may be times when there is nothing available which meets your needs or the needs of your pupils and you may need to produce something yourself. Most 'home-made' resources are worksheets of one type or another. These seem to be principally text, perhaps supported by diagrams or illustrations. A prime consideration with this type of material it that it should be readable. There are various reading age tests which give an indication of language level and teachers in the Special Needs department will give advice. Some word processors will calculate reading ages from passages of text using several different formulae. However, all these tests were first developed for assessing long passages of continuous text such as in fiction books. There is some doubt about their validity when used on shorter passages, particularly with a complex vocabulary as found in a science context. As mentioned earlier, the concept of readability goes beyond assessment of reading age and is much more complex. Research shows that layout and design issues can be far more important than language level in determining whether or not the reader can cope with the text. Motivation also plays an important part. Because there are so many variables involved, there are no comprehensive readability tests. Perhaps the best way to assess the readability of a resource is to give it to a potential reader!

Resource production is best undertaken as a collaborative activity. The involvement of Special Needs teachers could obviously be valuable particularly when resources are being developed for children with learning difficulties. Working with colleagues in the science department to 'shred' one another's work has been shown to be a good way of improving quality provided that it is done in a mutually supportive way!

As far as design and layout are concerned, few of us have had the opportunity for even basic training. Some teachers have an intuitive feel for what will work and what won't but many do not! It is possible to cheat a little by making use of the pre-prepared templates that come with many word-processing and DTP packages. There are also some straightforward pieces of advice about the design and production of print content resources which should be borne in mind. In line with the general theme of this part of this section, they are all expressed as don'ts!

☛ Don't ignore the importance of structuring. Is there a clear title? Are headings and sub-headings used appropriately to organise the content? Are diagrams and illustrations clearly labelled. It is clear why they are there? Could there be an advance organiser to summarise the overall content?

☛ Don't put in too much information. Is there any 'white space' on the page? Is the line length for text appropriate (not too long or too short) for the size of type? Is the overall effect visually attractive or too fussy? Is the information contained in the most appropriate form? Could a diagram or illustration convey meaning more clearly than words?

☛ Don't get carried away with the word-processor or desktop publishing software – limit the number of fonts you use (generally two or three should be the maximum). Use serif fonts (such as this one – Palatino, or Times) for text and san-serif fonts (like this one – Helvetica, or Monaco) for headings. Use *italic* or **bold** for emphasis of single words or phrases rather than underline and avoid UPPER CASE which many pupils find hard to read. Use boxes and/or shading ('screen') to highlight passages of text. Use 'bullet points' to summarise information – text should be left justified ('ragged right') rather than fully justified which provides no visual cues when the reader's eyes move from one line to the next.

☛ Don't forget to make sure that the language level matches the target user. This does not always mean writing as simply as possible – children will soon feel patronised if the material 'talks down' to them. Obviously, the language needs to be straightforward and as concise as possible. Scientific words will need explanation especially when introduced for the first time.

☛ Don't ignore the expertise of others. Are there Art and Design teachers with graphic design skills who could offer comments and ideas? It might even be possible to involve GCSE or A-level students in a project to redesign materials.

If you really want to know more about producing your own resources, then Rob Powell's book **'Resources for Flexible Learning'** *(Network Educational Press)* contains some straightforward advice drawing mainly on Roger Parker's **'Looking Good in Print'** *(Ventana Press)*, giving some practical examples of how to improve layout and design.

Management of resources

The central point argued above is that the whole process of choosing effective resources depends on how you are going to use them. If you are class teaching and want pupils to all use the same resource you obviously need a class set of textbooks, worksheets or whatever. If you try to think about more flexible use of resources and particularly about what can be gained by separating content from instructional information, it will be possible to use a wider variety of resources so that you might need fewer of each.

However, this does require a different view of classroom management as the probability is that pupils will be working on different materials at the same time. The message from the previous chapter is that perhaps our schemes of work should be supporting this by suggesting different routes through a topic, which in itself sets up the need for a more open and flexible approach to classroom management. The purpose of the next chapter is to look at the practical issues of classroom management in more detail.

REVIEW OF SECTION FIVE

- Are you using as wide a variety of resources – including IT – as possible to support your teaching? Are you able to make use of new resources on media such as CD-ROM?

- Do you make the most of the resources you have got? Does everyone know what is available to the department as a whole? Is there an effective storage and retrieval system?

- Is there an over-reliance on 'home-made' worksheets? If so, why is this? What could be done to improve the quality of this type of resource?

- Would there be advantages to the department in looking at separating 'content' from 'task' information when producing worksheets?

- What is the potential for developing some sort of 'task card' or 'study guide' approach to the classroom management of learning?

5.1 ———————————————————————— Reviewing resources

Purpose:
To analyse different types of resource material used in the department.

Activity:

1   Collect a range of different types of material used in the department (this could include worksheets, textbooks, reference books, industrial resources, etc.)

2   Read pages 73 to 74 about 'content' and 'instructional' information.

3   Identify examples of the two types of information in the materials selected.

4   Consider these questions in relation to the materials reviewed:

- How well matched is the content information to the needs of the pupils who will be using it?

- How well matched is the instructional information?

- Where a resource contains both types of information, could anything be gained by separating them, as suggested in Section Five?

- Are there any other ways in which the material could be modified to make it more effective?

Notes:
This could be an individual activity or members of the department could work in pairs. It might be sensible to concentrate on materials used with a particular year group or for a particular topic.

This activity is probably best focused on print medium resources, particularly worksheets and textbooks which combine both sorts of information. Other media (for example, video or posters) basically contain 'content' information. Another activity could be to consider how best to use this type of resource – i.e. how to provide 'instructional' information.

Readability ——————————————————— 5.2

Purpose:
To consider the concept of 'readability' and its assessment.

Activity:
1   Using the information on pages 79 and 80 and/or the sources suggested, read about the design and production of printed materials.

2   Try to agree on a definition for the term 'readability' and produce a list of factors which affect it. These can then be used as evaluation criteria for curriculum materials.

3   Take an existing resource, such as a worksheet and evaluate its readability using the criteria.

4   Rewrite the resource to make it more 'readable' by addressing the issues raised from the evaluation.

Notes:
This activity could stop after stage 3. Perhaps there will be enough value in the exercise by just evaluating the material without actually producing an improved version.

The book stresses that assessing readability involves more than a reading age test. However, such tests may be more important indicators where there are longer passages of text, as in reference books. There are a number of formulae which can be used to calculate reading age – **'Secondary Science – Contemporary Issues and Practical Approaches'**, *J J Wellington (Routledge, 1994)* p.177/8 for information about the most common ones. Microsoft Word 5.1 or later versions (and perhaps other word-processors) includes a reading age measurement (Flesch) which comes up after the grammar checker has been run but this requires the text to already be on disk, otherwise it will have to be typed or scanned in.

Teaching for effective learning

It was suggested at the end of Section One that if we are serious about planning for effective learning and responding appropriately to pupils' individual needs, it changes our perspective on the form and content of the schemes of work from which we teach.

In this section we will put forward some ideas about the practical issues of organising all of this in the science laboratory. We will do three things:

- **present an overall management framework**
- **consider the role of the teacher**
- **identify what preparation might be needed**

It has been difficult for schools in those parts of the UK faced with the very hasty introduction of a national curriculum (and then two equally hasty revisions) to do anything other than produce schemes of work that were essentially constructed to demonstrate coverage of the programmes of study and provide much-needed support to harassed teachers looking for some security in the form of a degree of prescription.

It is not surprising therefore that the end-products have been relatively inflexible, linear translations of the content into lists of activities. The only sort of planned differentiation here is limited to, for example, the suggested use of different resources for different sets. The basic principle which we challenge is that everyone should do everything.

In Section Four we considered how we might now move on, with the development of more flexible schemes of work built around an analysis of the content to show the way concepts were related and how ideas developed through it. From this, learning routes or pathways could be identified, perhaps in terms of learning outcomes for the pupils, and then consideration given to appropriate activities to achieve those ends.

Section Five then picked up on the selection and development of resources and explored the potential for a more open approach to thinking about their use. This raised the possibility of pupils working on different activities while using the same resources, at least for some phases in the teaching of a topic. The reasons for wanting to do this go back to some of the issues regarding effective learning discussed in Section One, and in particular to responding to learners needs on a more personalised basis.

A management framework

A scheme of work as described in Section Four is a strategic document. It defines goals but requires some decisions to be made about possible approaches to achieving them in order to put it into operation. The next stage could be in the hands of the individual teacher or be developed collaboratively by the department. It involves making decisions about classroom organisation and teaching approaches within some sort of overall **management framework** which provides a rationale for their selection.

Learning cycles

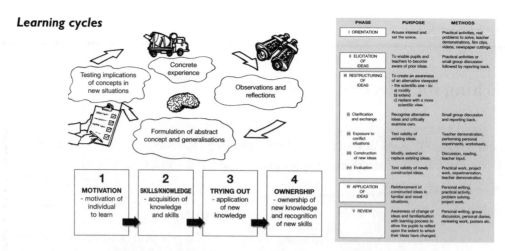

PHASE	PURPOSE	METHODS
I ORIENTATION	Arouse interest and set the scene.	Practical activities, real problems to solve, teacher demonstrations, film clips, videos, newspaper cuttings.
II ELICITATION OF IDEAS	To enable pupils and teachers to become aware of prior ideas.	Practical activities or small group discussion followed by reporting back.
III RESTRUCTURING OF IDEAS	To create an awareness of an alternative viewpoint - the scientific one - to: a) modify b) extend or c) replace with a more scientific view.	
(i) Clarification and exchange	Recognise alternative ideas and critically examine own.	Small group discussion and reporting back.
(ii) Exposure to conflict situations	Test validity of existing ideas.	Teacher demonstration, performing personal experiments, worksheets.
(iii) Construction of new ideas	Modify, extend or replace existing ideas.	Discussion, reading, teacher input.
(iv) Evaluation	Test validity of newly constructed ideas.	Practical work, project work, experimentation, teacher demonstration.
IV APPLICATION OF IDEAS	Reinforcement of constructed ideas in familiar and novel situations.	Personal writing, practical activity, problem solving, project work.
V REVIEW	Awareness of change of ideas and familiarisation with learning process to allow the pupils to reflect upon the extent to which their ideas have changed.	Personal writing, group discussion, personal diaries, reviewing work, posters etc.

In Section One we described some different learning models and their importance in effective learning. In Section Four we stressed the importance of having a learning model and linking the activities in the scheme of work to that model. These models of learning are also to some extent models for management. In his book **'Classroom Management'** *(Network Educational Press)*, Philip Waterhouse suggests a very similar management framework for the teaching of a topic:

An outline design for the teaching of a topic

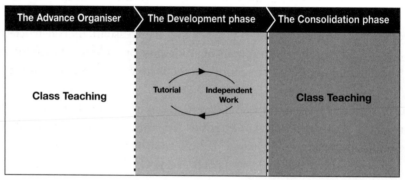

'Classroom Management' P Waterhouse (NEP)

It begins with an 'advance organiser' phase, predominantly with class teaching, leading into a 'development' phase which consists of several cycles of independent work by pupils individually, in pairs or small groups, alternating with tutorials with the teacher. The final 'consolidation' phase is also mainly through whole-class lessons to draw together key areas and provide opportunities to present work done.

Whether they have three, four, six or eight phases, these frameworks do not fit easily within the traditional lesson structure commencing with a fairly formal start, followed by some practical work or another sort of activity and then 'rounded off' at the end. They present a challenge to science lessons which are (perhaps because of the structure of a scheme of work) essentially self-contained. The sort of influences we looked at in Section One suggest that perhaps learning cannot always be confined into 70 to 100 minute units. Pupils may need longer periods, perhaps over several lessons, to work on activities, particularly if there is a more challenging outcome than completing a worksheet.

The use of a task card or study guide approach certainly implies a more extensive independent study phase than could be accommodated within one or two hours. Obviously there will be concerns about pupils remaining 'on task' and retaining motivation for longer periods of time when class teaching experience suggests that concentration spans are short, but this may be to do with the way the learning experience is set up and the degree of ownership that pupils feel.

Effective Learning in Science

The IDC cycle

Whatever sort of management framework you choose to adopt or adapt from those outlined here, it will probably share the common feature of them all in that it will have a beginning, a middle and an end. We could use the words 'Induction', 'Development' and 'Consolidation' to try to characterise the three components – the IDC cycle. It is practically impossible to find words which link accurately to all the models presented but perhaps these three convey something of the required meaning.

Our assertion is that the potential for meeting individual needs (and thereby addressing several elements leading to effective learning) will be increased by extending the timeframe of the IDC cycle.

Thus, if the IDC cycle only lasts for one block of timetabled time (a single or double lesson), the only approaches may be to use extension work or differentiated worksheets covering roughly the same content at different levels. If the cycle lasts for several lessons, the potential is increased – pupils could begin with a whole class lesson followed by two or three lessons working on a circus of differentiated activities, followed by a concluding lesson with a role play and discussion. Extend the timeframe even further and pupils could use a study guide to work through larger bodies of content with tutorial support at regular intervals.

Analysing how the length of the learning cycle meets the potential for satisfying needs

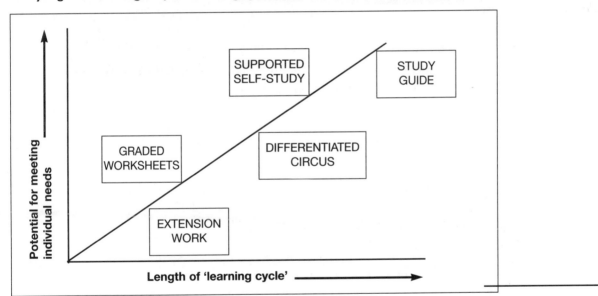

As we have already recognised, the stereotypical lesson structure has a beginning, a middle and an end which roughly correspond to the IDC phases. We are suggesting two developments. First, an overall increase in the time for the complete cycle; and second, a redistribution of time between the phases. Research from the CLIS project (see p.12) in particular reinforces the importance of allowing sufficient time for the 'I' and 'C' phases if childrens' learning is to be meaningful and persistent. 'D' activity without appropriate preparation and follow-up can have reduced effect.

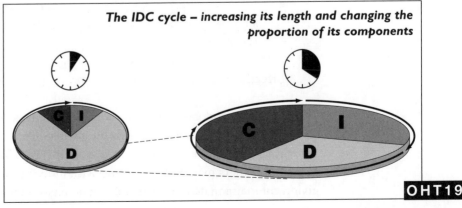

The IDC cycle – increasing its length and changing the proportion of its components

The decisions you make about the length of timeframe for this or whatever sort of management framework you use to put your scheme of work into operation seems to be crucial. Indeed, it will have implications for the structure and style of your scheme of work. Will it be divided up into short sections corresponding to individual lessons or will it be presented in a more open way to allow flexible interpretations?

Philip Waterhouse's book **'Classroom Management'** provides some very practical advice about the organisation and management of each stage in this sort of framework.

What is the role of the teacher?

The importance of the teacher is stressed in the report **'Science Education for Scottish Schools'** to which we referred in Section Two. It suggests that pupils' learning in science needs teachers who:

> - *are enthusiastic and knowledgeable about science*
> - *are confident about learning alongside the pupils they teach*
> - *provide positive role models of scientific curiosity, competence and creativity*
> - *encourage imaginative and personally original thinking*
> - *demonstrate openness, sensitivity and a willingness to take young people's ideas and questions seriously*
> - *are willing and able to deploy a wide variety of teaching strategies*
> - *have access to appropriate and adequately resourced opportunities for personal and professional development*

OHT20

Science Education in Scottish Schools Looking to the Future: A paper for discussion and consultation *(Scottish CCC, 1996)*

There is a good match with comments from students in Brian Woolnough's research into factors affecting success in producing scientists and engineers:

> - *Having teachers who are interested and enthusiastic about what they were teaching helped to develop my love of science and learning about science.*
> - *My physics teacher was a good teacher because she would try and relate physics to every day. The biology teacher was also quite good as she would take us out and try and relate things to the larger context.*
> - *In the third year I had a really good biology teacher. She was strict but she was nice. She really encouraged me and I started getting really good marks and I enjoyed it.*
> - *Good teachers notice when you're confused and they help you. They know exactly what's going on and explain well.*
> - *My physics teacher was extremely supportive, very enthusiastic and he'd say, anytime come and see me. I had extra lunchtime sessions and he was always available.*

'Effective Science Teaching', *B E Woolnough (Open University Press, 1994)*

There are many and varied reasons why we became science teachers but the desire to share the love of our subject with young people usually comes quite high on the list. There is some variation, however, as to how this is to be achieved: some enjoy the class exposition, others may prefer working with individuals or small groups; some enjoy giving entertaining demonstrations, others may prefer encouraging pupils' own investigations. There is room for a range of approaches, although we briefly considered in Section One whether there might be a not entirely healthy link between our preferred learning style and our predominant teaching style! In the light of the above discussion about management frameworks, there may, however, be some challenges to the role of the teacher.

As part of a study in Scottish schools, pupils were asked about what helped them to learn:

> [It] was not an individualised scheme or set of resources, not a particular form of grouping or set of activities, but a TEACHER – a teacher who was readily available and approachable, who noticed when they had difficulties, who took the time and trouble to give them explanations which they were able to understand, who paced the work appropriately, who set realistic goals for them both in the short and the long term, and who gave them good quality and timeous feedback on their performance.

'What's the difference?', *M Simpson & M Ure (Northern College, 1993)*

Effective use of the teacher's time is vital in effective learning. This will be true no matter what form of management system or classroom organisation is in operation. The key issue with any teaching approach is that the teacher can maximise the amount of time available in the lesson for high-level interactions with pupils rather than the lower-level 'management' interactions which can so easily dominate classroom time. This will apply when teaching the whole class as well as when adopting more individualised approaches. Philip Waterhouse discusses what he terms 'active class teaching' in his book '**Classroom Management**' *(Network Educational Press)* and suggests a number of strategies to involve as many pupils as possible in whole class activities. If pupils are working from a system using task cards or on a study guide, it should not be seen as replacing the teacher but actually freeing her or him to interact at a more individual level with the pupils. It is a strategy for gaining valuable pupil contact time during the lesson. This sort of freedom is precisely what we don't have most of the time when we are class teaching or when pupils are working on short-term activities – the best we can hope to do is keep them on task or help with relatively trivial questions. What we are aiming for is to increase opportunities for differentiation by support and response as proposed in Section One, or to use the term used by Richard Stradling and Lesley Saunders ...

> ... differentiation by dialogue, where teachers regularly discuss with individual pupils the work they are doing in order to interpret their understanding of it and to diagnose and review any emerging learning needs (not just difficulties).

'Differentiation in practice', *Educational Research 35 (2) 1993*

Avoiding the nightmare of becoming 'glue monitor' and not having opportunities for these more important conversations is largely down to the quality of your management framework and to thorough preparation – of yourself, of your resources and of your classroom, and of your pupils. With the right sort of preparation you can create time to be a learning manager rather than a resource manager.

Preparation

Assuming that decisions have been made about schemes of work and management frameworks, what preparation is required to put them into action? The detailed answer to this question will depend on exactly what sort of decisions have been made. The further you wish to go down the lines we have discussed, the more preparation will be needed. What follows is more of a checklist of points to consider, with some amplification of each. You will need to consider how far they apply to your situation:

1 Subject knowledge

One of the most important areas is your familiarity with the overall content of the topic. You will need to have a clear understanding of the possible routes through the material and of the resources available if you are to guide pupils into appropriate activities. You cannot operate on a 'one-step-at-a-time' basis – you need to be familiar with the learning outcomes and how these might be matched to different pupils in your class. The possession of the sort of subject knowledge described in Section Two as pedagogical content knowledge (PCK) is perhaps never more important than here. Of course, if you have been involved in the production of the scheme of work you will have been able to share PCK with others in the department and the scheme of work itself will provide you with quite a detailed map of the terrain showing possible routes and ways in which to differentiate the content. This will probably have suggested activities with relevant resources so it is not necessary to carry it all in your head but the detailed subject knowledge will be vital in any sort of 'tutorial' situation with individuals and small groups.

2 Pupil knowledge

The more information you have about your pupils, the more effectively you will be able to match pupils to activities where there are choices available through learning routes in the scheme of work. Developing this knowledge takes time and may require a review of record-keeping systems and the passing on of information from teacher to teacher. There are advantages here in teachers not changing groups from year to year in order to maintain continuity but this may conflict with policies of setting or grouping pupils. Again perhaps these need to be reviewed. It may also challenge the wisdom of the policy of rotating teachers in modular schemes, in that it is difficult to build up this pupil knowledge. (We do recognise the paradox here – the reason for having a rota is often to make most effective use of teachers' specialist subject knowledge!)

3 Grouping pupils

Detailed pupil knowledge will also inform decisions about grouping pupils whether in terms of setting or within classes. If there is a policy of setting, then perhaps it could be based on a wider range of performance indicators than just test or examination results. Within classes, generally pupils work (for example, for practical work) in friendship groups. These are not always the most productive groupings when social interactions interfere with learning tasks. Although there may be some consumer resistance, some teachers use other approaches such as giving pupils at random cards with names of chemical elements, or representatives of plant or animal groups. Then all the 'Halogens' or all the 'Amphibians' can form groups. Another approach could be to make up a set of cards with a number and a colour on them. Several different groupings are then possible – all the 1s, all the reds, a group of four different colours. Recent work with high-low ability pairs has shown advantages to both partners – the lower ability child benefits from tutorial support; the higher ability child consolidates understanding by providing it.

4 **Study and information skills**

If you are considering extending the timeframe for learning cycles to build in more independent work by pupils, it is important that they have the skills necessary to operate in what may be a new way of learning and understand how they are supposed to work. If they are to work on activities in study guides for example, then they may need to have experience in using one in a whole class lesson where everyone is working on the same activity but perhaps using different resources. Time invested in inducting pupils into a new approach can pay off in the longer term by them being more confident and capable of independent work, so leaving you to concentrate on supporting the learning rather than supporting the system.

5 **Your teaching room**

What can you do to organise your classroom for more effective learning? If you have an old-style fixed-bench laboratory, the answer is probably not much. But if you have a room with 'island' or overhead services, it does give some flexibility to look at room layout. There may be less need to arrange benches or tables for pupils to 'face the front' – what messages do they get about learning from this anyway? Think about the pupil movement around the room. Where will they need to go to get resources or equipment? Where will they need to go to see you? How can you make sure you have ease of movement around the room?

6 **Resources**

You need to think about storage of resources and equipment. Simple systems can be developed for making print resources available, but does your instructional material need to make clear where other sorts of resources are stored? Is equipment going to be 'trayed up' for each activity or will pupils be expected to collect it together for themselves? Again simple systems are possible. Rob Powell's book **'Resources for Flexible Learning'** *(Network Educational Press)* provides some practical ideas about selecting and storing resources.

It is vital to involve your technical support team in all of this. They may be able to see possibilities for the use of rooms and resources which you may not and they certainly need to be aware of the different nature of demand for practical equipment, for example.

7 **Monitoring and recording progress**

If, at some stages in the learning cycle, pupils are to work on different activities at their own pace the question of monitoring will inevitably arise – how do you keep track of what they are doing? The traditional mark book is not up to the job of maintaining a record of which activities pupils are working on, when they started it, when they should finish and any individual notes about targets and progress. Although the use of a computer-based system might suggest itself and could be quite easily developed, it is possible to manage this much more simply. The approach developed at the Bristol Resources for Learning Development Unit was to produce an A5 record card, one for each pupil.

Record card

NAME: JANET HODGES	CLASS: 2Q	ELECTRICITY

DATE	TASK	COMMENTS
12/1/78	2, 3	✓ Use correct circuit symbols. Good knowledge of house wiring circuits
16/1/78	7	← Try building your circuit. Use the bell in Tray 9
19/1/78	8	V. Good idea
23/1/78	11	Discuss scale readings
26/1/78	14	Excellent writing on new uses of elect. Well done
"	Test 1	─ Also wire up the light socket (Tray 6)
30/1/78	21	←

USE OF CIRCUIT BOARD	✓
SERIES & PARALLEL CIRCUITS	✓
CIRCUIT DESIGN	✓
AMMETER	✓
HEATING & FUSES	
WIRING A PLUG	
CONDUCTORS & INSULATORS	
ELECTRO-MAGNETS	
MAGNETISM	
CELLS AND BATTERIES	
VOLTAGE	
DIMMERS & RECTIFIERS	

HOMEWORK				TESTS	
1	7	6		1	8
2	8	7		2	
3	8	8		crossword	
4		9		Final Asses.	
5		10			

HODGES Janet | 1 X X 4 5 6 X X 9 10 X 12 13 X 15 16 17 18 19 20 X 22 23 24 25 26 27 28 29 30 31 32 33 34 35 36 37 38 39 40 |

... and finally

We would not want to end this section without making it clear that any emphasis on preparation associated with pupils being involved in more independent work should not be seen as suggesting that we are advocating a pendulum swing from class teaching to some form of resource-based learning. Effective learning requires a careful integration of a variety of different teaching approaches. Class teaching and whole class activities will have an important part to play as will more independent activities. The key selection criterion is the match between the teaching approach and the learning outcome or outcomes for the pupils, as we have emphasised throughout the book.

REVIEW OF SECTION SIX

- What 'management framework' is used in the department to provide the rationale for deciding approaches to be used in teaching?

- Is the management framework explicit (e.g. is it described in departmental documentation) or is it left to individual teachers to decide? Would there be benefits from sharing ideas about this?

- How are ideas about children's learning of science built into curriculum planning both at the level of schemes of work and individual lessons?

- What does the 'Induction-Development-Consolidation' (IDC) cycle look like in your department? Is it limited to an individual 'lesson' or does it extend across several?

- We emphasise the need for teachers to have good 'pedagogical content knowledge' (PCK). How can this best be developed and enhanced in the department?

Lesson management ——————————————————————— 6.1

Purpose:
To investigate frameworks for managing learning used in the department.

Activity:

1   Read the first part of Section Six (pages 85 to top of 88).

2   Collect appropriate evidence to build up a picture of classroom management approaches used in the department – is there anything about this in the Science Department Handbook? What do the schemes of work say about teaching and learning approaches?

3   Consider these questions:

- Do lessons have the 'IDC' structure presented in the book?
- What is the 'timeframe'? Is it limited to 70-100 minutes?
- Does the structure of lessons relate to any ideas about childrens' learning in science?
- Would there be value in thinking about a more extended timeframe?
- What implications would this have for lesson planning and preparation?
- How could the practical problems be addressed?

Notes:
The 'data collection' in stage 2 could be limited to departmental documentation or could extend into some classroom observation to see what happens in practice. This could prove a valuable insight into the range of approaches to managing learning which are in use in the department.

The issue addressed by the questions in stage 3 is about the potential for more effective learning through lengthening the timeframe for the learning cycle, as discussed in Section Six. This could also be achieved by a 'force field analysis' exercise which presents individuals with a grid:

1 **Advantages**	2 **Reinforcement**
3 **Disadvantages**	4 **Counter-measures**

They complete the grid in relation to what they see to be the advantages (1) and disadvantages (3). For the advantages, they think what might be done to reinforce them (2) and then for the disadvantages, what might be done to overcome the problems (4). Individuals can then compare their ideas.

6.2 ——————————————————— The role of the teacher

Purpose:
To consider the role of the teacher in effective learning.

Activity:

1   Read pages 88-89, particularly the set of bullet points listing characteristics of good science teachers.

2   Select the three which you think are the most important and the three least important. Compare with colleagues in the department. How much agreement is there between you? Are there other characteristics which you would want to include in the list?

3   You could use the list or produce a list of your own to reflect on yourself as a science teacher. How do you match up to these ideals? What are the associated professional development needs?

4   Read through pages 90-91 about preparation. Are there areas here which individuals or the department as a whole might address?

Notes:
Stage 2 could be to consider whether staff agree or disagree with these statements rather than select the most and least important.

The suggestion in stage 3 is obviously a sensitive area to explore. This could be a bit of personal reflection for members of the department rather than an exercise which everyone shares at a department meeting or where the Head of Department attempts to assess colleagues! Handle with care!!

Some sort of prioritising exercise in stage 4, either by individuals or at departmental level, could lead to the identification of targets for the department's development plan.

Afterword

Where to now?

In this book we have tried to bring together a number of ideas about what characterises effective learning in science. We have looked at the issue from the learner's viewpoint and explored how it relates to the content of the science curriculum. This led us into an audit of current practice as a way of identifying possible areas for action. The following three sections considered planning and teaching for effective learning, providing sources of ideas for departmental developments. The picture that emerges is of a complex inter-relationship of factors but the key points relate to our four aims:

- to help departments integrate into their practice a number of different influences on what effective learning looks like;

- to argue for a more sophisticated approach to developing schemes of work that have greater potential to match learners' needs;

- to show that ideas about effective learning are easier to address if we move away from dividing our teaching up into short 'lessons' and towards thinking about 'learning cycles' within a longer timescale;

- to encourage science departments to exploit the professional development opportunities in a collaborative approach to curriculum planning.

In the Appendix we have included some ideas for activities to be done through individual or collaborative work in department meetings or on in-service days. We hope that these will help to develop a shared vision of where the department is going and indicate areas for development. In the Bibliography we have included some useful references to more detailed advice and further reading but from here on it is up to you how things move forward.

Our advice would be that the next logical step is to produce some sort of development or action plan. It may be that the initial interest in this area has arisen from a School Development Plan priority or from the Action Plan produced in response to a school inspection. The production of an action plan is quite straightforward once you have decided on the action! It is then mostly just a case of agreeing who will do what, by when and with what resources. The most difficult part is deciding on what you are going to do when there is such a range of possibilities:

- Are we going to review and revise schemes of work?
- If so, which topic are we going to start with?
- Shall we increase the range of resources used in the department ... ?
  ... or re-organise the way they are managed?
- Are we interested in introducing a different classroom management framework?
- Do we want to introduce more opportunities to build on childrens' ideas?
- Can we try to identify pupils' learning styles?

Some sort of prioritising activity may well be necessary to check whether there is a consensus in the department about an initial focus or whether pairs or small groups identify their own targets. The important thing is that everyone is aware of what everyone else is doing; that they are all clear about timescales and outcomes; and that, even if everyone is not doing the same thing, it is possible for everyone to feel a commitment to the exercise. We have stressed the value of collaborative action.

This is not only to do with ownership of the development (something which has been sadly lacking in much recent curriculum innovation) but because of the increased opportunities for the enhancement of pedagogical content knowledge, which we have emphasised in relation to effective teaching. With the removal of inter-school and local authority infrastructures for teachers to learn from one another, and reduced subject-oriented professional development opportunities with higher education institutions, departments must look for intra-institutional possibilities. The Head of Science has a crucial role in exploiting talent and expertise within the department in the most effective way. Hence our emphasis on acting collaboratively and the synergy this can produce.

We wish you well; take it slowly and remember the elephant – don't risk indigestion or worse by trying to bite off more than you can chew!

Bibliography

In writing this book we have tried to refer to a number of books and other publications which have contributed to our understanding of what makes for effective learning in science. Our intention here is to provide some suggested reading which might form the basis for a science department library (where funds exist for such luxuries!). This is a personal list and is certainly not a comprehensive survey of everything that is available about secondary science teaching. We have included recent publications which have influenced our thinking about the issues raised in this volume and which are clearly linked to classroom practice. They are not in an order of importance, but are grouped around particular themes. We hope they will be useful as sources of further reading and illumination.

Secondary Science: Contemporary Issues and Practical Approaches
Jerry Wellington (Routledge, 1994)
This wide-ranging book touches on almost all the themes we address – children's learning in science, language issues, differentiation, etc. Very helpfully, each section concludes with 'References and Further Reading' to take you more deeply into any of these.

Science Today: Problem or Crisis
Edited by Ralph Levinson & Jeff Thomas (Routledge, 1997)
A collection of contributions from scientists and science educators which takes a step back to consider 'real science', 'school science' and their relationship. There are interesting articles from Guy Claxton and Robin Millar. Very useful in thinking about what sort of science children should learn and why.

Making sense of secondary science: research into children's ideas
Rosalind Driver, Ann Squires, Peter Rushworth & Valerie Wood-Robinson (Routledge, 1994)
A comprehensive review of practically every topic you might teach in science to identify research into the pre-existing ideas which children may have and which have implications for their future learning. (A companion volume of Support Materials is also available.)

Young people's images of science
Rosalind Driver, John Leach, Robin Millar & Phil Scott (Open University Press, 1996)
Looks at children's ideas about science itself, making some important points about the future shape of the science curriculum.

The Differentiation Book: a guide to differentiation in secondary science teaching
Edited by Mick Revell (Northamptonshire Inspection & Advisory Service, 1995)
A really practical look at differentiation in science. Full of ideas on planning and developing schemes of work and differentiation strategies in the classroom.

Differentiated Science Teaching
Keith Postlethwaite (Open University Press, 1993)
A very detailed look at pupil differences and how to respond to them in the classroom. Clearly focused on meeting the needs of the individual through, for example, approaches such as Mastery Learning.

Differentiation: a practical handbook of classroom strategies
Chris Dickinson & Julie Wright (National Council for Educational Technology, 1993)
Based on work supported by the NCET, this booklet is not science specific but does contain a useful general model for thinking about differentiation and suggests a number of strategies for achieving it.

Differentiation in the secondary curriculum: debates and dilemmas
Edited by Susan Hart (Routledge, 1996)
Arose from an in-service course where teachers from a number of subject areas got together to try to make sense of 'differentiation'. Contains a number of relevant case studies and a useful chapter on learning styles by Michael Fielding.

Differentiated Primary Science

Anne Qualter (Open University Press, 1996)

Although it is obviously aimed at Key Stages 1 and 2, this book discusses issues which are highly pertinent to secondary science, indeed we may gain valuable insights and a different perspective by looking at them through the primary school context.

Practical Science

Edited by Brian Woolnough (Open University Press, 1991)

Raises some interesting and provoking questions about the nature and purpose of practical activities in encouraging effective learning in science.

Exploration: a way of learning science

Anne Qualter, Juliet Strang, Peter Swatton & Robert Taylor (Blackwell, 1990)

Based on work carried out by the Assessment of Performance Unit, this book presents a way of children learning science through practical exploration. Contains a useful section on progression in science and the relationship between procedural and conceptual understanding.

Investigative Work in the Science Curriculum

Richard Gott & Sandra Duggan (Open University Press, 1995)

Again, draws heavily on APU research to present a detailed blend of theory and practice concerning investigative work in science. As with the previous book, some useful material on progression and assessment.

Skills and Processes in Science Education

Edited by Jerry Wellington (Routledge, 1989)

Although 'pre-National Curriculum', this book provides some useful background reading when reviewing purposes of teaching science and planning for the future.

Explaining Science in the Classroom

Jon Ogborn, Gunther Kress, Isabel Martins & Kieran McGillicuddy (Open University Press, 1996)

An interesting book bringing science educators together with specialists in discourse and communication. It has a lot to say to science teachers about the way in which we present science to children and how we transform our own subject knowledge in the classroom.

Information Technology in Science and Technology Education

Jon Scaife and Jerry Wellington (Open University Press, 1993)

As we begin to grapple with the potential for IT to enhance both class teaching and more individualised approaches, this book provides ideas about effective use of IT and includes some practical examples.

Science Education for a Pluralist Society

Michael Reiss (Open University Press, 1993)

Explores the way school science education should be appropriate to the needs of all children. The emphasis is on challenging the often narrow, 'male' and Western view of science presented to children and the resultant alienating (and demotivating) effect this may have. It collects together a wide range of practical curriculum ideas for broadening and enriching science teaching.

Effective Science Teaching

Brian Woolnough (Open University Press, 1994)

This book too challenges the often impersonal way in which science is presented to children. Based on the author's research, it develops a strong argument for project work in science allowing learners to explore issues of relevance to them.

Finally, the three earlier publications in *The School Effectiveness Series* from Network Educational Press (**'Accelerated Learning in the Classroom'** by Alistair Smith, **'Effective Learning Activities'** by Chris Dickinson and **'Effective Heads of Department'** by Phil Jones & Nick Sparks) are all highly relevant to the management and delivery of effective learning.

Appendix

What do you believe about effective learning?

Mark each statement according to whether you agree, disagree or are undecided about it. It will then be analysed to look for patterns across the department.

	AGREE	UNDECIDED	DISAGREE
1 Pupils who are pro-active or take responsibility for their learning will become effective learners			
2 Those pupils who respond well to questions at the end of the lesson indicate that effective learning has taken place			
3 Effective teaching will lead to effective learning			
4 There are many approaches to learning; some are more effective than others			
5 Effective learning only occurs when the teaching style coincides with the pupil's preferred learning style			
6 Low ability pupils will never be effective learners			
7 Pupils should be free to learn in the way they think is most effective for them			
8 Effective learning takes place when teachers have a clear/coherent theory about how pupils learn			
9 Effective learning takes place when pupils' ideas are challenged			
10 When pupils know the targets they will learn more effectively			
11 Effective learning will take place when practical is used to illustrate theory			
12 Pupils' own ideas get in the way of effective learning			
13 Pupils will become effective learners if their teachers are effective learners			
14 Pupils can be taught how to learn effectively			
15 Teachers have implicit personal theories about how effective learning occurs			
16 Learning to learn effectively is a skill that can be acquired			
17 Pupils learn most effectively when they are allowed to absorb the content passively			
18 Encouraging pupils to ask questions will enhance their ability to learn effectively			
19 Effective learning is more likely to occur if teachers promote the development of pupils' thinking skills			
20 Questions that encourage hypothesising will produce more effective learning			

Cut out these statements and then, with a partner, try to group the statements under whatever headings you think are appropriate. You may be asked to put them onto a poster to show how you have grouped them.

Pupils who are pro-active or take responsibility for their learning will become effective learners	Effective learning will take place when practical is used to illustrate theory
Those pupils who respond well to questions at the end of the lesson indicate that effective learning has taken place	Pupils' own ideas get in the way of effective learning
Effective teaching will lead to effective learning	Pupils will become effective learners if their teachers are effective learners
There are many approaches to learning; some are more effective than others	Pupils can be taught how to learn effectively
Effective learning only occurs when the teaching style coincides with the pupil's preferred learning style	Teachers have implicit personal theories about how effective learning occurs
Low ability pupils will never be effective learners	Learning to learn effectively is a skill that can be acquired
Pupils should be free to learn in the way they think is most effective for them	Pupils learn most effectively when they are allowed to absorb the content passively
Effective learning takes place when teachers have a clear/coherent theory about how pupils learn	Encouraging pupils to ask questions will enhance their ability to learn effectively
Effective learning takes place when pupils' ideas are challenged	Effective learning is more likely to occur if teachers promote the development of pupils' thinking skills
When pupils know the targets they will learn more effectively	Questions that encourage hypothesising will produce more effective learning

Reviewing schemes of work

Does the SoW currently:	Yes	No	Action to be taken
● Provide an overview/links with NC?			
● Show how the content has been analysed?			
● Identify the major concepts and show how they are related to one another?			
● Identify previous knowledge/concepts/skills required?			
● Make learning objectives and success criteria explicit?			
● Show learning pathways through tasks and activities?			
● Show conceptual progression?			
● Show where formative assessment should occur?			
● Point out where children usually experience difficulty?			
● Give typical pupil misconceptions?			
● Show how assessment framework reflects relative emphases placed on skills, knowledge and understanding?			
● Identify safety issues/relevant Hazcards?			
● Show links with children's lives outside school/links with industry?			

- to help departments integrate a number of different influences in picturing what effective learning means for them

- to argue for a more sophisticated approach to developing schemes of work that have greater potential to match learners' needs

- to show that ideas about effective learning are easier to address if we move away from dividing our teaching up into short 'lessons' and towards thinking about 'learning cycles' within a longer timescale

- to encourage science departments to exploit the professional development opportunities in a collaborative approach to curriculum planning

---

OHT2   A CONSTRUCTIVIST VIEW OF LEARNING

- Learning outcomes depend not only on the learning environment but also on the knowledge of the learner.

- Learning involves the construction of meanings. Meanings constructed by pupils from what they see or hear may not be those intended. Construction of a meaning is influenced to a large extent by their existing knowledge.

- The construction of meaning is a continuous and active process.

- Meanings, once constructed, are evaluated and can be accepted or rejected.

- Learners have the final responsibility for their learning.

CLIS, University of Leeds

- Producing posters to answer questions such as "How does electricity flow round a circuit?"

- Making concept maps to show relationships between ideas about how plants feed

- Sorting cards with names of common substances into piles of solids, liquids and gases

- Completing questionnaires about which human characteristics can be inherited

- A circus of simple practical experiments to investigate floating and sinking

- control of variables, and exclusion of irrelevant variables

- ratio and proportionality

- compensation and equilibrium

- classification

- probability and correlation

- use of formal models to explain and predict

OHT4   A CONSTRUCTIVIST MODEL FOR TEACHING

PHASE	PURPOSE	METHODS
I ORIENTATION	Arouse interest and set the scene.	Practical activities, real problems to solve, teacher demonstrations, film clips, videos, newspaper cuttings.
II ELICITATION OF IDEAS	To enable pupils and teachers to become aware of prior ideas.	Practical activities or small group discussion followed by reporting back.
III RESTRUCTURING OF IDEAS	To create an awareness of an alternative viewpoint - the scientific one - to: a) modify b) extend or c) replace with a more scientific view.	
(i) Clarification and exchange	Recognise alternative ideas and critically examine own.	Small group discussion and reporting back.
(ii) Exposure to conflict situations	Test validity of existing ideas.	Teacher demonstration, performing personal experiments, worksheets.
(iii) Construction of new ideas	Modify, extend or replace existing ideas.	Discussion, reading, teacher input.
(iv) Evaluation	Test validity of newly constructed ideas.	Practical work, project work, experimentation, teacher demonstration.
IV APPLICATION OF IDEAS	Reinforcement of constructed ideas in familiar and novel situations.	Personal writing, practical activity, problem solving, project work.
V REVIEW	Awareness of change of ideas and familiarization with learning process to allow the pupils to reflect upon the extent to which their ideas have changed.	Personal writing, group discussion, personal diaries, reviewing work, posters etc.

CLIS, University of Leeds

Dynamic learners ...

- like to try things out and don't worry about getting it wrong
- enjoy variety and look for excitement
- are keen to take action and get others involved
- don't want to plan and don't want to check work
- manage their time badly

Common sense learners ...

- read instructions carefully and organise their time well
- enjoy solving problems by integrating theory and practice
- work well alone, are thorough and decisive
- like doing things their way but are not very imaginative
- want to get the job done but don't like being given answers

Imaginative learners ...

- like to see the whole picture and see relationships between ideas
- enjoy brainstorming sessions and using their imagination
- listen well and like group work
- work in fits and starts and forget important details
- are easily distracted and indecisive

Analytic learners ...

- are well organised and can work alone
- are analytical and logical and see links between ideas
- set clear goals and apply theories to problems
- don't like group discussion
- get bogged down in detail

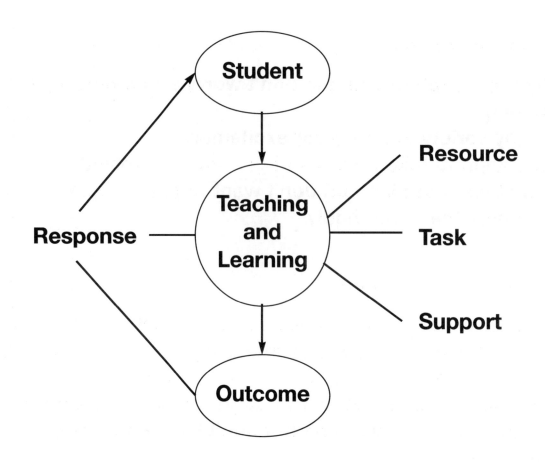

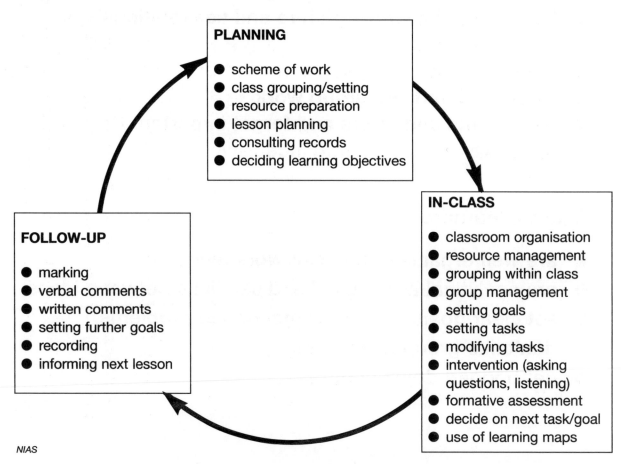

- ... there are opportunities to build on children's own ideas

- ... there is a clear relationship between procedural and conceptual understanding

- ... teaching approaches recognise that pupils learn in different ways

- ... activities are related to pupils' needs

- ... pupils 'know where they are going'

- ... pupils are given appropriate challenges

- ... pupils are well motivated and have positive attitudes

- ... prior learning is recognised and valued

Competence can be improved through the practice of skills and through the application of knowledge.

Coping skills can be developed through experience of handling problems facing one's self and society.

Creativity can be promoted through tackling open-ended as opposed to closed problems.

Co-operation can be developed through experience of working in teams.

An important dimension of developing capability is giving young people greater responsibility for their own learning.

G Bell (RSA)

- the first sort is the traditional concept to do with the amount of knowledge we have – knowing *that;*

- the second sort is about using our knowledge and skills so that we know what to do in particular situations – knowing *how;*

- and the third sort is, as Claxton puts it – 'knowing what to do when you don't know what to do'!

- An enquiring habit of mind – *scientific curiosity*

- Ability to investigate scientifically – *scientific competence*

- Understanding of scientific ideas and the way science works – *scientific understanding*

- Ability to think and act creatively – *scientific creativity*

- Critical awareness of the role of science in society combined with a caring and responsible disposition – *scientific sensitivity*

SCCC, 1996

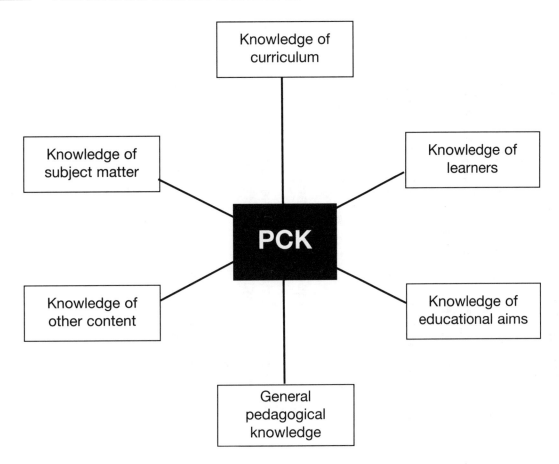

Adapted from work by J Calderhead (Cassell Educational)

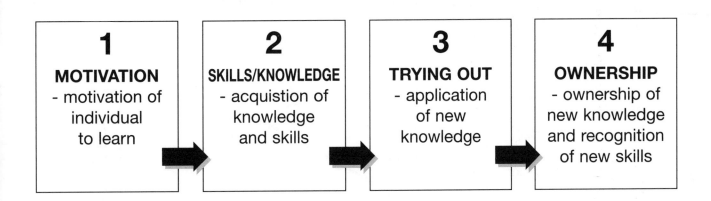

Adapted from work by G Bell (RSA)

- They allow a more selective approach to the use of resources.

- They can be customised to the needs of the school (for example, regarding equipment).

- Consumable worksheets provide a paper record of work done by pupils.

- They may be a cheaper alternative to textbooks.

- They take to a lot of time to produce yourself.

- There is considerable variation in final quality.

- There is a limit to the use of colour, which makes them generally unattractive compared to textbooks.

- They often involve copyright infringements regarding illustrations and photographs!

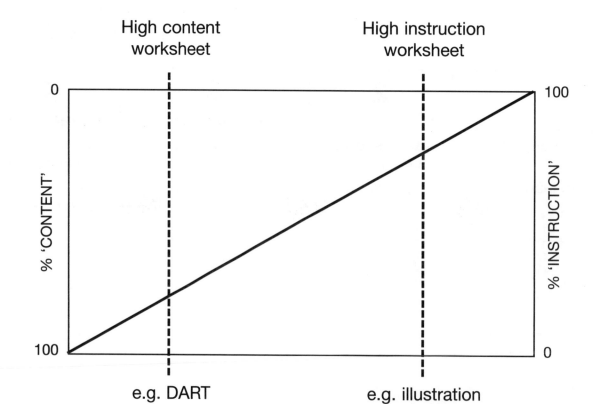

- The use of advance organisers to present aims and learning outcomes clearly.

- A list of suggested resources is provided which could be added to or customised before the guide is photocopied for use.

- The guide has 'white space' to allow pupils and teachers to add additional information to define, clarify or extend tasks.

- The tasks themselves are presented in challenging ways which require pupils to research the topic for themselves rather than just answering a series of questions.

- The guides contain a number of prompts to help pupils get started and work through the activities.

- The activities are designed to generate some sort of 'product' but this is not always the normal sort of written account. It could be an oral presentation, a report designed for a particular audience, or even a video.

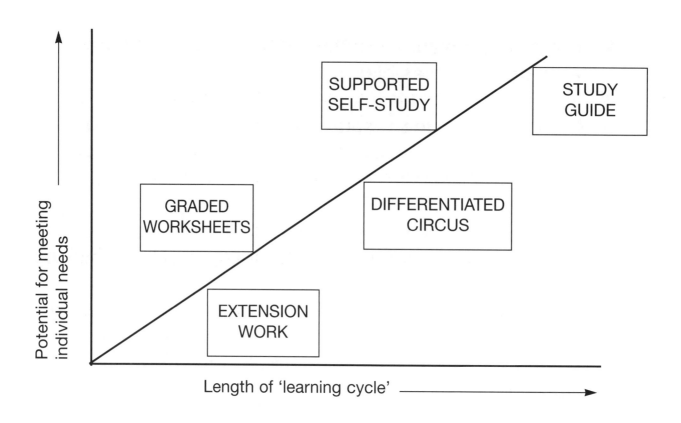

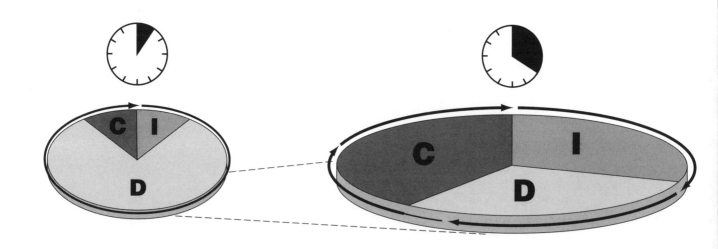

WHAT IS THE ROLE OF THE TEACHER?

- are enthusiastic and knowledgeable about science

- are confident about learning alongside the pupils they teach

- provide positive role models of scientific curiosity, competence and creativity

- encourage imaginative and personally original thinking

- demonstrate openness, sensitivity and a willingness to take young people's ideas and questions seriously

- are willing and able to deploy a wide variety of teaching strategies

- have access to appropriate and adequately resourced opportunities for personal and professional development

Science Education in Scottish Schools (Scottish CCC, 1996)

Effective Learning in Science is the fifth title in The School Effectiveness Series, which focuses on practical and useful ideas for school teachers. This series addresses the issues of whole school improvement along with new knowledge about teaching and learning, and offers straightforward solutions which teachers can use to make life more rewarding for themselves and those they teach.

Book 1: *Accelerated Learning in the Classroom* by Alistair Smith
ISBN: 1855390345   £15.95

- The first book in the UK to apply new knowledge about the brain to classroom practice
- Contains practical methods so teachers can apply accelerated learning theories to their own classrooms
- Aims to increase the pace of learning and deepen understanding
- Includes advice on how to create the ideal environment for learning and how to help learners fulfil their potential
- Full of lively illustrations, diagrams and plans
- Offers practical solutions on improving performance, motivation and understanding
- Contains a checklist of action points for the classroom - 21 ways to improve learning

Book 2: *Effective Learning Activities* by Chris Dickinson
ISBN: 1855390353   £8.95

- An essential teaching guide which focuses on practical activities to improve learning
- Aims to improve results through effective learning, which will raise achievement, deepen understanding, promote self-esteem and improve motivation
- Includes activities which are designed to promote differentiation and understanding
- Offers advice on how to maximise the use of available - and limited - resources
- Includes activities suitable for GCSE, National Curriculum, Highers, GSVQ and GNVQ
- From the author of the highly acclaimed Differentiation: A Practical Handbook of Classroom Strategies

Book 3: *Effective Heads of Department* by Phil Jones & Nick Sparks
ISBN: 1855390361   £8.95

- An ideal support for Heads of Department looking to develop necessary management skills
- Contains a range of practical systems and approaches; each of the eight sections ends with a "checklist for action"
- Designed to develop practice in line with OFSTED expectations and DfEE thinking by monitoring and improving quality
- Addresses issues such as managing resources, leadership, learning, departmental planning and making assessment valuable
- Includes useful information for Senior Managers in schools who are looking to enhance the effectiveness of their Heads of Department

Book 4: *Lessons are for Learning* by Mike Hughes
ISBN: 1855390388   £11.95

- Brings together the theory of learning with the realities of the classroom environment
- Encourages teachers to reflect on their own classroom practice and challenges them to think about why they teach in the way they do
- Develops a clear picture of what constitutes effective classroom practice
- Offers practical suggestions for activities that bridge the gap between recent developments in the theory of learning and the constraints of classroom teaching
- Ideal for stimulating thought and generating discussion
- Written by a practising teacher who has also worked as a teaching advisor, a PGCE co-ordinator and an OFSTED inspector